WIRED TO GROW

Harness the Power of Brain Science to Master Any Skill

Britt Andreatta, PhD

7th Mind
Publishing

7th Mind
Publishing

This edition April 2016
Seventh Mind Publishing
Santa Barbara, California

For speaking engagements please contact Jacqui Sneathen at Speaking@BrittAndreatta.com, or visit www.BrittAndreatta.com.

For order or bulk purchases of this book, please write Orders@7thMindPublishing.com.

Printing by Dog Ear Publishing
www.dogearpublishing.net

ISBN: 978-0-9973547-1-3 (paper)
ISBN: 978-0-9973547-0-6 (ebook)

This book is printed on acid-free paper.

Printed in the United States of America.

For Chris and Kiana.

I am so blessed to share this life with you.

TABLE OF CONTENTS

Introduction

Take a Learning Journey

I. Neuroscience

II. Phase 1: Learn

III. Phase 2: Remember

IV. Phase 3: Do

V. Design

INTRODUCTION

I think learning is the most powerful and natural process in the world. Learning is at the heart of any transformation we have made or will ever make both as individuals and a society.

I am not talking about education or training but the process of learning: how we start at one level of awareness, understanding, or skill and shift to a different—and better—level.

We are biologically wired to learn. Our survival depends on our ability to learn from our environment and experiences. And therefore, intrinsically, several aspects of our central and peripheral nervous system are dedicated to the learning process. Thousands of years ago, when all humans were living in tribes and subsisting off the land, our ancestors who survived were the ones who learned how to recognize when predators were nearby, which foods were poisonous, and how to read signs of hostility in others.

Today, our survival instinct still drives much of our learning but the context is vastly different. Instead of learning how to forage for food, we must successfully navigate our work environments. Survival is still the goal, since we use our paychecks to buy food and shelter. But rather than learning to build fires and shelter, we now need to know how to drive and use computers.

Socially, we still need to develop emotional intelligence in order to read signs of hostility in others, as well as kindness, curiosity, and a host of other complex emotions. While that need hasn't changed, we now need to do it beyond the familiarity of a shared language, culture, or geographic region. And we might even use emotional intelligence to understand words on a monitor, a voice on a device, or a face on a two-dimensional screen.

In addition to being the key to our survival, learning is also the path to fulfilling our potential—our capacity to become or develop into something more than we are. Within each of us is unrealized ability waiting to blossom into the fullest expression of who we are meant to be.

As individuals and as a species, we yearn to become more, to realize the highest and best version of ourselves. It's in our DNA, the strands of which even visually model the journey of an ever-upward climb. *Wired to Grow* is designed to help fully unlock potential by understanding the neuroscience of learning and how to maximize our ability to learn and grow. You can apply this material to your own life immediately, starting today. If you have a role where you help others learn and grow, you will gain new tools for unlocking their potential as well, becoming a more effective manager, parent, leader, educator, or health care worker.

So how did this book come about? I work at the intersection of leadership and learning, often helping leaders figure out how to maximize the potential of their organization and the people within it. In addition to my own intellectual curiosity, I am an active practitioner in the field. Every week, I am designing and delivering learning experiences to adult professionals to solve some of today's biggest business challenges.

As I seek to improve my craft, I continuously explore the latest empirical studies by current researchers and thought leaders in a range of fields, including neuroscience, biology, psychology, education, and even anthropology. To be clear, I am not a neuroscientist; my PhD is in education, leadership, and organizations, and I have done my own research on what makes people successful. I find and review scientific studies and have a knack for connecting the dots within and between different disciplines. And, analyzing the latest research, it became clear that a variety of studies across a wide range of fields were telling a similar story. I began to map them and I found incredible parallels. And because I am an active practitioner, designing and delivering learning experiences out in the field, I also got to see where lab studies were and were not translating to how people experience learning out in the real world.

What I found not only changed how I design and deliver learning for others but also how I approach my own transformation. Now that I know and truly understand the neuroscience of learning, I have unlocked more of my own potential and the potential of participants in my sessions.

I am handing these keys to you as well.

So let's take a journey together. I'd like to introduce you to the fascinating miracle that happens inside of you every day. And once you understand this process, you will be able to use it more effectively and efficiently in your own life and help others apply it as well.

Take a Learning Journey

Before I wrote this book, I taught this content through workshops, keynote presentations at conferences and corporations, and an online training course on Lynda.com. In a live presentation, I model these concepts so participants get the most out of the experience. I'd like to replicate that for you here, so before you read on, pick something that you'd like to learn. It could be something you are currently learning, or something you want to learn in the near future. It could be a new professional skill, like public speaking or mastering unfamiliar software. Or it could be something personal like playing an instrument, speaking a new language, or dancing the tango.

The only requirement: it should be truly meaningful to you.

As you work through the book, apply each concept to this thing you want to learn, and by the end you will have a robust and exciting plan to help you realize your potential in this area. To help you, I have created a free downloadable PDF for you to print and fill out as you explore each concept (www.BrittAndreatta.com/Wired-to-Grow).

Tip: If you really want to maximize your experience, find a partner to share with. As you will discover in chapter 12, social learning actually boosts long-term retention. So find a friend interested in chatting with you about what you learn in this book and your progress on your learning object. Perhaps they might want to take this journey with you, comparing notes as they learn something new themselves.

I. NEUROSCIENCE

When we learn, visible changes actually take place in the brain. In fact, some researchers want to *define* learning as an event that creates a physical change in the brain. Neuroscience studies how the biological features of our central and peripheral nervous system work together to create and retain new knowledge and skills. As you'll see, the latest neuroscience research coming out of places like Harvard, Stanford, University of Wisconsin, and New York University is driving a whole new understanding of our inner workings. Beyond neuroscience, a host of other disciplines study how the brain shapes human thought and behavior including psychology, psychiatry, and anthropology.

1. Advances in Brain Science

Advances in medical technology now allow researchers to see inside brains and bodies at a microscopic level and they can observe what is happening in ways they never could before.

Cue image from childhood movie favorite, *Fantastic Voyage*, when a blood clot threatens the brain of an important scientist, and a miniaturized medical team travels inside his body to repair his brain. As they zoom through his bloodstream, they see the inner workings of the scientist's body in larger-than-life, Technicolor clarity. In the coming pages, we'll be traveling the brain to reveal its inner workings and how to use its own nature to enhance learning and learning design. From the greater insight learned through research, we now know that different parts of the brain play different core roles in the stages of learning, starting with how a person first takes in new information, then stores that information into memory, and finally uses it to create real and lasting behavior change.

These findings have exciting implications for every level of education, as well as training, and development in every sector and industry. And it's imperative that learning professionals keep their finger on the pulse of brain science. If we don't work *with* the brain and its natural processes, even the most popular or highly rated learning programs won't deliver in the long run. As researchers learn more about how the brain and nervous system work, the information gleaned continues to enhance the quality of the learning experiences they design for children and adults alike.

Three Important Brain Structures

The three most important brain structures involved in learning are the hippocampus, the amygdala, and the basal ganglia.

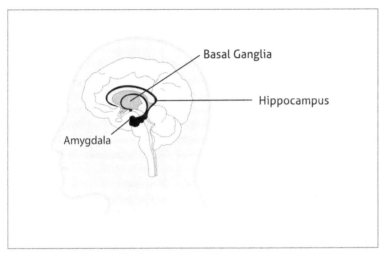

Key brain structures for learning

The hippocampus is located in the center of our skull and has prongs that extend into both the left and right hemispheres, essentially uniting the brain. It is physically attached to the amygdala, the structure that is most recognized for its role in our survival through the fight, flight, or freeze response. How we learn and how what we learn is placed into our memory is the hippocampus's responsibility. All of our major sensory nerves—optical, aural, olfactory—feed directly in to the amygdala. When the amygdala is aroused, the hippocampus automatically turns on.

And finally, the basal ganglia is responsible for taking common, routinized behaviors and turning them into habit loops. Anything you do that used to take a lot of effort or focus but is now second nature—

for example, driving your car or using a new smart phone—is evidence of the basal ganglia's role.

We will learn more about how these structures work in upcoming chapters.

Other key players in the learning process: neurons (cells that communicate through electrical and chemical signals) and the neural pathways they create (a series of neurons linked together for a specific activity or thought). These communications occur at the end of their tendril-like extensions, called synapses. They exist throughout our body and are involved with every human function from thinking and feeling to moving.

Scientists can now actually see and measure how these cells thicken with use. The more a neuron or neural pathway is used, the stronger it becomes, much like a bicep muscle does when we work out. And this encompasses all learning, both cognitive and behavioral.

The important implication here is that what we think and do matters. With every choice we make, we are strengthening neural pathways. We can strengthen the pathways of happiness and joy or that of judgment and frustration. We can strengthen healthy actions like exercise, play, and mindfulness, rather than reinforcing mindless eating, distraction, and overwork.

Positive psychologists have discovered that things we used to assume were personality traits, like happiness and resilience, are actually just neural pathways that any of us can develop. If you want to learn more, check out the works of Dr. Brené Brown, author of *The Gifts of Imperfection*, and Dr. Shawn Achor, who wrote *The Happiness Advantage*.

2. The Growing Brain

A key discovery in brain science is that the brain is incredibly flexible. It can grow and change over our lifetimes, an ability known as neuroplasticity. These findings have debunked the long-held belief that our brain is static. In fact, our brain can and does change all the way up until death.

This means that it's never too late to learn something new. Shifting your ideas and worldviews as well as your skills and behaviors can be a game changer. In terms of learning, it means that you are no longer stuck with ideas you formed about yourself as a child and young adult.

For example, if you decided or were told that you are bad at math or not good with people, brain scientists would tell you that it's not true. While you may not have well-developed neural pathways in those areas, you can absolutely change them by starting to use them and developing them. And here's a critical component of brain health: We must treat our brain much like we treat our muscular body. We can challenge it to try new things and as we practice those new things, we will get better and stronger. Websites like Luminosity are designed to do just that, providing the brain with mental workouts to keep it flexible and healthy.

Neuroplasticity supports the work of Stanford University psychologist, Dr. Carol Dweck, who wrote the book *Mindset: How We Can Learn to Fulfill Our Potential.* Dweck's research explored achievement and success and found that people tend to have either a fixed or growth mindset. In other words, they have differing beliefs or worldviews about how we learn and grow.

People with a fixed mindset believe their traits or characteristics—such as their IQ (intelligence quotient) or people skills—are set once they reach adulthood. A person with a fixed mindset thinks, *I've got what I've got and I just have to make the most of it, but I can't change it.* In contrast, a person with a growth mindset believes that they can always get better, that they can always learn something new, or practice something more, and that studying and effort are the pathways to improvement and even mastery. A person with a growth mindset thinks, *I may not be able to do this yet, but I can work hard and get better.* In fact, the word "yet" is the hallmark of the growth mindset. The recent findings on neuroplasticity have proven that flexibility is in fact the truth of our brains.

This is what I find incredibly exciting: neuroscience is proving that we don't have to be stuck with what we were taught to believe about ourselves. You can still become good at math or better with people or learn a new language. Wherever your skillsets are now, you can do something to make them better. All kinds of organizations, from schools to businesses, are embracing this concept and looking for ways to activate the growth mindset in folks with a fixed mindset.

And, research is showing it's possible. A study in high school students, by Dr. Ruth Butler, a professor of educational psychology, broke participants into two groups and gave them all an exam split into two parts: questions 1 to 5 and questions 6 to 10. Remember the traditional bell-curve test-taking model from school? Where performance is compared to the others' in class, and rank is assigned relative to the highest and lowest scores? In this particular study, the first group was told that their whole test would be compared to the group. When asked to speculate why, students described the purpose of relative grading as to "show how good you are." See what their speculation revealed there? Comparisons activate the fixed mindset.

The second group was given different information: They were told they would be taking the same exam in two parts, but that they would be compared to themselves. In other words, their performance on questions 1 to 5 would be compared to how they individually did on questions 6 to 10. When asked to suggest what the purpose might be, the students said, "to show improvement," which is essentially the growth mindset of getting better.

The results were really fascinating. On the first part of the exam, questions 1 to 5, both groups did about the same. Their scores were statistically identical. Then something remarkable happened. On the second part of the exam, the students who were compared to the others in the group did about the same as the first part. There was no noticeable improvement. But guess what happened to the group that was told that improvement mattered? Their performance improved! And not by a little, by a lot.

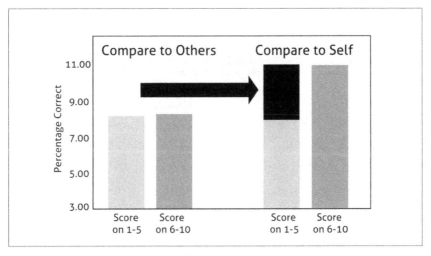

The value of measuring improvement

In the table, the black zone shows the growth mindset. When people are told that growth matters, they step up and they improve. To me, that black box means potential. Those students had unrealized ability in their knowledge of the material. And it wasn't more studying that brought it out, but rather the motivation that comes from knowing that improvement matters.

The growth mindset yields all kinds of other benefits too. Look at this comparison of how mindset influences everything, from how we view effort, challenges, and feedback to the success of others.

Fixed Mindset	Growth Mindset
leads to a desire to look good, so tends to:	*leads to a desire to learn so tends to:*
Believe that most skills are based on traits that are fixed and cannot change	Believe that skills can always improve with hard work
See effort as unnecessary; something to do when you're not good enough	See effort as a path to mastery and therefore essential
Avoid challenges because could reveal lack of skill; tends to give up easily	Embrace challenges and see them as opportunity to grow
See feedback as personally threatening to sense of self and gets defensive	See feedback as useful for learning and improving
View setbacks as discouraging; tends to blame others	View setbacks as a wake-up call to work harder next time
Feel threatened by the success of others; may undermine others in effort to look good	Find lessons and inspiration in the success of others
As a result, they may plateau early and achieve less than their full potential.	**As a result, they reach ever-higher levels of potential and performance.**

The two mindsets at work

While this was an academic study, we know the same dynamic applies to performance evaluations, too. A lot of organizations are rethinking their performance review processes, moving away from ratings, and instead focusing on growth and improvement.

When we rate people in any setting as "average," "excellent," or "poor," we essentially replicate the fixed mindset and say, *You are what you are.* But when we move to evaluating growth and improvement, we activate motivation and ultimately potential, saying, *You are what you reach for.*

In my consulting work, I have helped some global companies shift their performance reviews to create a growth mindset. In them, an employee who is struggling to meet goals will receive the message "not yet" rather than being "poor" or "below expectations." That shift signifies so much: the person has potential and the organization has faith that they can improve. We are finding that this positive, aspirational expectation is far more likely to motivate an employee to grow than being labeled substandard.

But does it really matter to activate the growth mindset? Not everyone can get straight As or be promoted to the top positions, right? While it might be true that rewards are limited to top performers and that some organizations need to control access to certain rewards, leaders can also use a process in which rewards are proportionately distributed, and growth and improvement are measured along with performance. These and similar changes are revolutionizing today's work environments.

While people with the growth mindset achieve ever-higher levels of potential and performance, the organizations they work for reap the benefits of that as well. Remember, the growth mindset is actually the truth of human nature. So now the challenge is getting folks who hold the fixed mindset to shift their worldview to align with their potential.

We can certainly do this with children. As a parent, Po Bronson and Ashley Merryman's book *Nurture Shock: New Thinking about Children* changed my world, showing me how we can cultivate mindsets in our children by how we parent them. Complimenting them based on traits—"Honey, you are so smart"—instills a fixed mindset. But when we compliment them for their improvement and effort—"Honey, you worked really hard on that and look how it paid off"—we instill a growth mindset. (Learn more at www.nurtureshock.com.)

For more astounding brain science, *The Whole-Brain Child* by neuropsychiatrist Daniel Siegel, MD, and Tina Bryson, PhD, has parents and educators around the world rethinking how we approach learning and engaging children. Dr. Alan Kazdin, from Yale University, has built an entire method of parenting, including how to deal with "difficult" behavior, from growth mindset and related perspectives.

And Sal Khan, the founder and creator of the Khan Academy, created a website where students of all ages can watch simple videos on math and science. He has shown the validity of neuroplasticity and the growth mindset by analyzing the data of people learning on his site. You can see that one student grasps the content quickly and zooms through the material, while others might watch a video several times before accurately answering questions. Regardless, when they have the *aha!* moment and start to really understand the material, you can see the spike in speed and comprehension. And when that moment happens, the student just skyrockets. Their scores go through the roof. Khan's whole academy and learning service is based on these ideas: that you can get better and that the *aha!* matters.

Kahn's data clearly shows that when they study material online, people benefit from controlling their own pace and honoring their unique needs. They can pause and rewind material as many times as they need without having to raise their hand, risking judgment and ridicule from their peers or the teacher. We know that the social dynamics among children (and, frankly, adults too) can hinder people from asking for the help they need but that all disappears when people can pace themselves.

As you manage your personal learning goals, remember the mantra of the growth mindset: *yet.* You may think, *I don't know how to do it* yet. Or, *I'm not good at it* yet, *but I can be.* So let's embrace the *yet,* and figure out where it is that you want to go with the things you want to learn.

3. The Three-Phase Learning Model

Learning is *the* acknowledged pathway to improvement, so it's natural that as organizations seek to improve their people they look to new programs and techniques to enhance it. But too many initiatives are not designed as effectively as they could be. The premiere corporate learning research firm, Bersin by Deloitte, conducts annual studies on the latest trends in learning and talent development. Their data shows that corporations are spending more money on learning and development than ever before. And yet many researchers now believe as much as 90 percent of new skills learned are lost within a year. If learning activities don't yield real and sustainable behavior change, that investment is wasted.

Because brain science ranges across many disciplines (neurology, biology, psychology, and so on) and each researcher has a fairly specific and narrow focus (memory, brain injury, behavior, and so on), there is no one centralized place to look for how brain science might inform learning professionals.

As a result, as one of those learning professionals seeking cutting-edge information in learning and development, I have immersed myself in neuroscience research, which has forever changed how I approach learning design and delivery. Some of the studies confirmed things I had found through trial and error long ago; others completely shifted how I approach my craft.

When I create any learning program, I first figure out the content that the session will cover. This is the actual information or skills we hope the learner will learn. Then there is the learning delivery or the actual learning event itself, and how that event is constructed through options like discussions, hands-on application, lecture, etc. Finally, there is the behavior we want after the learner leaves the session, as all learning seeks to change either someone's knowledge or behavior, and often both. (In professional settings the focus is almost always on behavior change of some kind.)

Informed by the research, I created my own three-phase learning model, simple and straightforward, in support of the functions it describes:

1. Learn
2. Remember
3. Do

The first phase—Learn—is self-explanatory. A learner takes in new information in some way, and understands it. The second phase—Remember—is about retaining what she learned. Learning something today but forgetting it tomorrow, doesn't do much good. But even if remembered, the learner ultimately has to do something with it, which takes us to Phase 3: Do. This phase is about behavior change and using what is learned to do something out in the real world.

All three phases are equally important to really bring about change. In the next chapters, I will walk you through how to get the most out of each—both in your own life or your efforts to cultivate change in others.

Your Learning Journey

As mentioned, in each chapter I'll remind you to give these concepts a try in your own life. In each of the next three sections, take the thing you want to learn and consider how you might maximize your learning.

II. PHASE 1—LEARN

Let's start with the first phase, which is how we actually absorb and integrate new information. Here are three things you should know about the Learn phase:

- learning happens in levels,
- learning happens in a cycle, and
- focus is super-important.

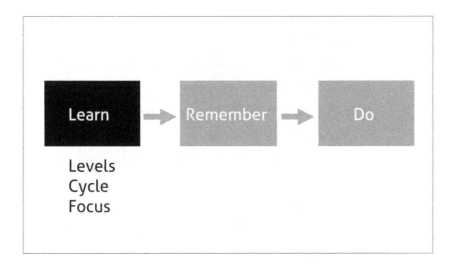

4. Learning Grows Up

Before we jump in to the specifics, let's first examine how adults learn. While we often associate learning with childhood, in fact, we are biologically wired to continually learn from our environment and experiences, otherwise our species wouldn't prevail. Learning occurs throughout our lifetimes.

Alexander Kapp, an important theorist of adult learning, from Germany, created the concept of *andragogy*, how adults learn, in contrast with *pedagogy*, how children learn. An American educator, Malcolm Knowles, built upon Kapp's work and helped to integrate it into the humanistic learning theory, which first described learning as a means to fulfilling potential, and was developed by luminaries such as Abraham Maslow and Carl Rogers.

Knowles (1984) identified five key assumptions of adult learners that make their learning different from children:

1. As we grow, we become more independent from our families of origin. This allows us to become self-directed in what we learn and also gives us our unique self-concept.
2. As we live longer, we accumulate a base of knowledge and experience, which becomes a resource for learning as it grows. For example, you may have an *aha!* moment today that connects to something you read five years ago or something that happened in your last job.
3. As independent adults we have many responsibilities, and this actually increases our readiness to learn because we are seeking to solve real-life challenges. This makes learning much more salient for us.
4. Our orientation similarly shifts to finding solutions to our day-to-day problems rather than the more abstract learning

we did as children. When we seek learning as adults, it's often to solve a current problem.

5. Our motivation to learn becomes internalized. While we are born learners, the structure and pressure of school often casts learning as a duty or responsibility. Being forced to learn every day according to the school districts' plans often diminishes love of learning. As adults we can reclaim that internal motivation and learn something simply because it interests us.

These assumptions led Knowles to identify some key principles for working with adult learners (1984), which are still much used by learning designers:

- Learning materials should honor the wide range of backgrounds and experiences that learners bring with them, and be designed to work for different skills levels, learning styles, etc.
- Learning should allow learners to discover things for themselves through self-directed experiences. And, making mistakes should be considered an important part of the learning process.
- Learning should be contextualized for how the learner will actually apply the information to their lives, including understanding the "why" behind what is being taught.

Frankly, this list works for children too but sadly, it's often not applied in our school systems. Good teachers seek to create engaging and empowering environments but the sheer size of their classes, coupled with rigid goals from district, state and federal agencies make it challenging. Many alternative school systems for children do seek to empower independent learning rather than force a rigid education plan upon them, most notably the Montessori and Waldorf systems. In my opinion, if we truly focused on learning in our schools, rather than education, we would better prepare people to become the thoughtful citizens, leaders, and parents that we want them to be.

5. Knowledge Has Levels

Bloom's Taxonomy of Knowledge (1956) is another theory related to the Learn phase. This model has stood the test of time because it tapped into neuroscience principles before we really knew what they were. Dr. Benjamin Bloom discovered that all knowledge is not the same, and that different levels of knowledge mean different levels of learning too.

The most basic level is memorization: rote repetition of what is told to you. For example, a child can recite, "Two plus two equals four" without knowing what it means. The next level up is comprehension, or understanding. ("I am doing addition here. I can add three plus five and get eight.") The next level up is application, where you take what you learned into a new context. In this case, you would take math and use it in real life. ("I'm going to use addition and subtraction to balance my checkbook.") These first three levels are often the hallmarks of K–12 education and work with all subjects. For example, you can memorize history, you can truly comprehend the forces that led to different historical events, and you can apply that knowledge to current events. And you can experience all of it through assignments like writing a paper or taking a test.

The next three levels—called higher-order thinking—are the hallmarks of higher education and professional learning. You're taking that base knowledge and doing something new with it. Some people rank these levels but I believe they are equally complex. One of the higher levels is analysis, where you take something apart. For example, you could use math, in this case statistical calculations, to analyze a host of data. You could also sit down and look at your recent months of business to analyze your top-selling products and figure out where your customers live. Another level is evaluation, which requires you to judge something using some specific criteria. For example, you could evaluate your business using key performance indicators (KPIs) like customer satisfaction, profitability, and environmental impact.

Finally, we have creativity, which is taking information and doing something completely new with it. You might take what you learned about production processes and reengineer them. Or you might innovate a new way of thinking about leadership or providing a service.

The following figure shows the six levels of Bloom's Taxonomy and how the higher ordered thinking skills of analysis, evaluation and creativity rest upon a bedrock of memorization, comprehension and application.

CREATION	EVALUATION	ANALYZATION
Integrate and combine ideas to create a new product, plan, or proposal.	Appraise, assess, or critique on a basis of specific standards to justify a decision or course of action.	Differentiate, classify, and relate the assumptions, hypotheses, evidence, or structure of a statement or question.
Actions: Design, Invent, Produce, Hypothesize, Plan, Compose, Formulate, Generalize	*Actions: Judge, Recommend, Critique, Justify, Assess, Rank*	*Actions: Compare, Contrast, Organize, Categorize, Authenticate*

APPLICATION
Select, transfer, and use data and principles to complete
a problem or task with a minimum of direction.

Actions: Use, Compute, Demonstrate, Construct, Complete, Illustrate, Modify, Experiment

COMPREHENSION
Comprehend, explain, or interpret
information based on prior learning.

Actions: Explain, Illustrate, Exemplify, Predict, Summarize, Paraphrase, Discuss

MEMORIZATION
Remember or recognize information, ideas, and principles
in the approximate form in which they were learned.

Actions: Write, Label, Name, Define, Show, Describe, Identify, Recognize

Levels of knowledge

So the first phase of my Learn-Remember-Do model asks you to evaluate which explicit levels of Bloom's taxonomy you need for your learning objective. Most working adults need learning experiences that address all six levels to provide them with a robust set of skills. But sometimes it's challenging to work through them quickly, so you may choose to focus on one or two per learning event and then build up over time.

Applying Levels in the Real World

Let's look at an example of how to use Bloom's levels to maximize professional learning. I teach leadership, and one of the skills that is relevant to today's leaders is change management. All leaders need to know how to facilitate effective change in an organization. To help them, I look at Bloom's Taxonomy and make sure that I design learning that covers every level.

I begin by teaching leaders various models of change. We know some things about how people and organizations change, so I first make sure they understand these principles. Then I have them apply those theoretical models to a real change they are designing or leading so that it fits their current context, such as the skill sets of their team and their organization's structure and culture. Then I want them to determine if it's working. Very rarely do "models" roll out in the real world like they do in studies, so the ability to analyze how it's going and identify possible pinch points and solutions is critical to the success of any change initiative.

This is where creativity comes in. Perhaps the model isn't an exact fit for their context. Maybe they need to tweak it or combine two models to make it work better or to make something really unique and effective. Ability to innovate and think creatively are essential here, as are the skills to help others do the same.

Once the change is implemented, then it's time to determine the return on investment, or ROI, for that change, to evaluate it in metric terms that are relevant to the specific organization.

6. The Learning Cycle

Another model that has tapped into elements of neuroscience is Kolb's Learning Cycle. Created by Dr. David Kolb in 1984, this model maps learning against two continuums. First, you have the axis of perception that ranges from conceptual or abstract on one end to concrete experience on the other. The second axis is the processing continuum, which ranges from observing someone else to doing it yourself.

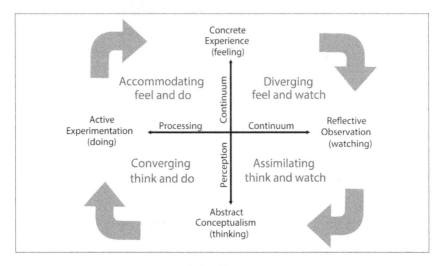

Cycle of learning

Kolb identified that good learning actually takes the learner through all four quadrants. You can jump in at any point on the model, but learning designers should mindfully take the learner through the entire cycle and the intersections of the perception and process continuums.

If we revisit my example from the previous section on teaching change management, learning about models of change is on the abstract-conceptual end of the perception continuum, while applying them to a project or team is on the opposite, concrete-experience end. As leaders roll out a change, they might be reflective and observe how it's going, perhaps doing some analysis and, if it's not unfolding smoothly, actively experiment with new solutions. Finally, evaluating the ROI of the change gets back to abstract again, so the learner has had the opportunity to move through all of the quadrants.

Clearly, Bloom and Kolb's models have some intersections between them as well. When research done at different times by different people lines up, I pay attention. It tells me something significant is happening. As we continue with the three-phase learning model, you will see that both Bloom and Kolb tapped into the neuroscience of learning and how our brains and bodies are wired to learn through doing.

7. Focus Feeds the Hippocampus

Learning only happens when the hippocampus, the part of the brain that takes in information and moves it to our memory, is functioning normally. When it's damaged, people lose access to past memories and can no longer make new ones. The hippocampus is the path by which any learning first enters the brain—the first stop on a long and complex journey—and it works in a consistent, predictable way. In fact, many learning challenges start because so often people don't work with how the hippocampus is designed to function.

The hippocampus acts like a recorder or data drive and, just like those devices, it has an "on" button. Physiologically, when our eyes and ears attune to something—in other words, when we focus—it causes the hippocampus to begin recording. Dr. Richard Davidson of the University of Wisconsin calls this "phase locking," and it's the starting point of all learning.

Without focus, we can't capture that important data, so it can't continue the process of being moved to memory or driving behavior change. This is why it's important to design learning environments to help people focus, and to bust the myth that you can multitask while learning. Research has proven that when we divide our attention, our focus actually switches back and forth between the two activities, also known as switch-tasking. I call this "swiss-tasking" because when switching back and forth, the hippocampus loses key pieces of information for each object of attention and we end up with holes in the data, and therefore irreversible holes in our learning. The hippocampus is physically incapable of recording two complete tracks of data simultaneously, so you must give learning the attention it deserves.

For example, if you have the TV on while you are trying to read this, your brain will go back and forth with your attention. If you focus on the TV for a few seconds, your brain can't really pick up the words

---

you are reading. And likewise, if you start to really focus on my words and their meaning, the TV will fade in to the background.

Multitasking carries two significant risks: First, we kid ourselves that we can do two things well. This may be true for certain activities—I can absolutely wash the dishes and listen to music—but when trying to learn, you must be able to focus. Second, the hippocampus is affected by those around us. Studies have shown that learners who are trying to focus on something are negatively affected by their neighbor who is multitasking. I've coined the term "second-hand distraction" to describe this phenomenon. And it's almost as dangerous as second-hand smoke in terms of the health of your learning.

Don't Max the Hippo

Another attribute of the hippocampus is that, again like any data drive, it can only hold so much information before it maxes out.

Now, if I was in the room with you, I would ask you to pause and guess how many minutes you think that is. If you want to play along, just cover the paragraph below with your hand for a minute. How long do you think the brain can focus before it needs a break to process what it just learned? Another way to think about this is to just remember the last time you sat in a class or listened to a webinar or read a book for learning. How long before you felt kind of saturated?

When I ask this in a presentation, I hear everything from one hour to five minutes. Here is the big shocker about the hippocampus . . . you ready? Studies show that the maximum amount the hippocampus can hold is about twenty minutes of information. Yep, twenty minutes. After that, it starts to write over the data already captured. So you may sit there for longer, but the learning you did at the beginning of the twenty minutes starts to drop off the recorder.

Despite being the overwhelmingly pervasive approach to learning, lecture-style sessions (think school and college) have never demonstrated good retention results and now we know why. Sitting for hours and trying to learn works against the brain's natural functioning. Our brains are meant to learn in short bursts of focus, which we can string together.

Here's the good news: All the hippocampus needs is a few minutes of processing to push that data into short-term memory and it's ready again for more. And, fortunately, learning activities can be designed to work *with* the brain's natural processes. I now build all my learning events in fifteen-minutes chunks of information, followed by a processing activity, like a discussion with a partner, a moment of private reflection, an experiential activity, or even a break. I then string these mini-modules together into a longer session, like an hour or two or three—although I rarely go longer than a half-day now because of what I have learned about the brain's need for time away from learning for reflection (more on this in chapter 12).

Since adopting this approach, I have seen a real increase in the effectiveness of learning events in terms of comprehension, retention, and, ultimately, behavior change.

It has also changed how I approach my own learning. Having gone through both a master's and a doctorate program, I have spent more than my fair share of hours in lectures, half-day seminars, full-day programs and trying to read really dense material that doesn't have the benefit of a leading character or a storyline. I always knew that after a certain point I wasn't retaining information but I thought it was because I just needed to work harder than other people.

Not so.

All this time, we have been designing education around a business delivery model, ignoring how the brain actually learns. When people start tuning out or getting restless, it's not necessarily because they are bored. It's because they are full. There is a difference.

So now I honor my brain function, and when I want to learn something I do it in bite-size chunks and then stop and process that information so it can go into memory. Then I fire up the old hippocampus by focusing and start again. I am astounded by how much more effectively I learn now that I work with my hippocampus. And learning is not the only activity that benefits from focus. Daniel Goleman's latest book *Focus: The Hidden Driver in Excellence* details the positive impact focusing has on leadership, decision-making, and creativity. And it makes sense. If focus is what kicks off key parts of our nervous system, it's the gateway to all kinds of important skills and abilities.

Do Write Your Notes

One more thing helps the hippocampus push learning into short-term memory, and that's the effort we spend while learning. Taking notes does actually help with learning because it adds another sensory element beyond our eyes and ears. It makes it more kinesthetic. Even more fascinating, hand writing notes is measurably better than typing them. With the advent of laptop computers, it's increasingly common for people use their computers for taking notes in class. But, it turns out, while we can type faster than we write we actually retain more of what we learn when we handwrite notes.

A series of interesting studies by researchers at Princeton University and UCLA compared students who took handwritten notes to those who used a laptop. The laptops only contained word processing software and were not connected to the Internet to minimize distraction. And they found over and over again that the students who handwrote their notes had better short-term *and* long-term retention of the material. They discovered that when people type, because it is so much faster, they end up transcribing the lecture verbatim. Since handwriting is slower, students had to do some mental heavy lifting by summarizing key points and organizing the material.

After this discovery, researchers ran more studies where they explicitly told the computer notetakers to focus on summarizing rather than typing verbatim. But despite these instructions, the students were seemingly unable to help themselves from transcribing the speakers' words. And in reality laptops do come with endless opportunities for distraction, and many of these, like the Internet, photos, and music, can easily create a switch-tasking experience that splits focus and hampers the hippocampus' ability to record the learning data.

These findings have been replicated by other researchers and map to my own experience. And mine is not the only one. A client of mine, a writer who interviews people for her work, has found that when she takes notes on her laptop, she doesn't retain what a person says. But when she takes notes by hand, she remembers details, and retains more information longer than when she types.

Do Your Doodles

Doodling is another surprisingly powerful type of notetaking that affects learning.

Yes, I said doodling.

Sunni Brown, author of *The Doodle Revolution: Unlock the Power to Think Differently*, calls doodling "applied visual thinking." Several studies back up her position, showing that visual note-taking boosts both retention (by up to 29 percent over non-doodlers) and also drives enhanced creative thinking.

Doodling is not just goofing off—it's actually "making spontaneous marks to help yourself think." This is because our brains are designed to be visual. Our species existed thousands of years before we even created written language and cave drawings show that our earliest forms of written communication were through images. The ancient doodle.

Sighted child's growth process demonstrates the power of visual learning: A baby can learn what a cat is and point to a picture of one months before she can say the word *cat*. And she can say *cat* years before she knows her letters and learns that C-A-T is the written representation of her furry friend. When we consider the complexity of different languages and discover that there is also *gato* (Spanish), *chat* (French), *kitte* (Arabic), and *neko* (Japanese)—well, it's no wonder our ancestors drew pictures.

The human brain often grasps understanding of visual information much more quickly than the same concept explained in words. Just imagine putting together your IKEA furniture if they wrote out the instructions in paragraphs instead of those cool pictographs?

I think this is why the Animate video series by RSA (the Royal Society for the Encouragement of Arts, Manufactures and Commerce) are popular. They animate meaningful voice recordings that help visually emphasize the main points. We not only hear the information but also see the concepts brought to life before our very eyes. As a learning designer, I sometimes leverage the power of doodling by showing the RSA versions of my favorite TED talks rather than the talks themselves, such as Dan Pink's "Drive," Brené Brown's "Empathy," and Jeremy Rifkin's "The Empathic Civilization" (see links in the Resources section). Now, Brown would argue that watching someone else doodle does not have the same kinesthetic power of doing our own, and she is right. But I have found that adding visual elements still augments learning in powerful and entertaining ways.

Sunni Brown states that doodling is a form of mental processing, so it not only aids in focus, it can help the hippocampus move information into short-term memory. By taking notes that are a combination of doodles (visual) and key words or phrases (linguistic), we actually lever-age more neural pathways as we tap into those regions of our brain.

So the next time you are learning, think twice before grabbing your laptop, unless you happen to have a drawing tablet attached to it. Grab your Sharpie and see what happens when you handwrite notes and doodles.

Your Learning Journey

Take a moment now to apply the concepts from this chapter to your learning journey. Use these questions to help you identify possible strategies to support your goals:

- How might you design your learning experience to work with the hippocampus? Consider how you can enhance your focus, as well as learn in fifteen- to twenty-minute segments with pro-cessing activities.
- What levels of Bloom's Taxonomy will you need to explore? And how can you design a learning experience that tends to the four quadrants of Kolb's Learning Cycle?
- How can you use handwritten notes and doodling to maximize your learning?

III. PHASE 2—REMEMBER

Let's go on to the second phase of learning, which is Remember. It's not enough to be exposed to new information, you need to be able to recall it in the future. If you learn something one day but then forget it, the learning experience is essentially wasted.

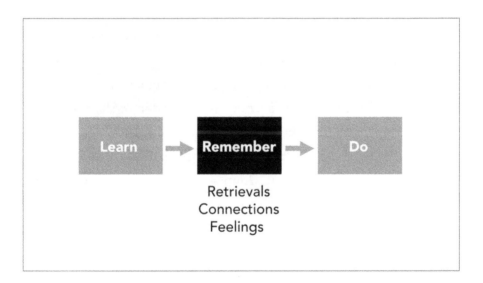

The goal is to get what you learn into long-term memory so that it's there for you to use when you need it even several months later.

8. Three Kinds of Memory

Let's first explore the different kinds of memory.

First, we have sensory memory, which is short-lived and basically includes what you notice with your senses, like the temperature of the room, the noise outside, or the warmth of your coffee mug. Even if you are not aware of it, your sensory memory processes thousands of sensations per day but you may not even register them unless something is unusual. For example, if you grab your coffee mug and it's cold when you were expecting warmth, you might notice it for a second as you head to the microwave.

Second, someone might draw your attention to something. Try this right now: Just tune in to the sounds in the room around you. What do you hear? Is there a hum from a machine or appliance? Can you hear sounds from outside like traffic or birds? What about your heartbeat or your breathing? Can you get quiet enough to hear them? Both noticing the coffee mug and tuning in to the sounds in the room activated your short-term memory. Also known as *working memory*, the hippocampus is involved in this kind. Just by focusing on sounds in the room, your "hippo-cam" turned on and started recording.

Third, all of us can recall with crystal clarity moments like car accidents, muggings, and fires even if they happened years ago and it all turned out fine. That's an example of *long-term memory*. Long-term memories are actually stored in the brain in a way that is retrievable over time. While short-term memory has a shelf life of minutes, long-term memory can literally be for a lifetime.

According to neuropsychologist Dr. Richard Mohs, studies have shown that long-term memory decays very little and that the brain is capable of storing an unlimited amount of information. This is because long-term memories involve the firing of neural pathways and synapses in much wider regions of the brain, compared to short-term memories that only occur in the frontal, prefrontal, and parietal lobes.

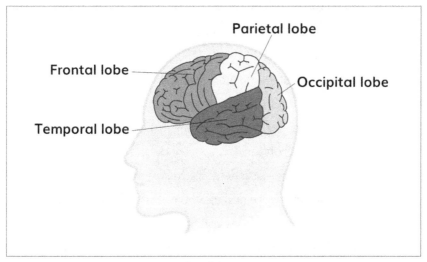

Lobes of the brain

The neural pathways of long-term memories are different from other memories, and this is something we can utilize as we explore our own learning. You can intentionally use brain science to take short-term memories and move them into long-term memory. Our body does this naturally with life-threatening moments but it can occur many other ways. As we learn more about this natural process, think of how you can use this information to drive your learning.

9. The Path to Long-Term Retention

Converting memories into the long-term sort is a three-fold process of retrieval, connections, and emotions. This means that you can take any information recorded by the hippocampus and intentionally push it into long-term memory.

Oh, if I had only known some of these tricks in college! Actually, brain scientists would tell me that much of what I learned in college is still sitting in my long-term memory. It's just the path to retrieving it has become obscured from disuse.

It's a like walking across a field. Pathways that are walked over and over again become well-worn and easy to retrace. For example, many of the things I still remember from college, like some theories of education and models of leadership, I used repeatedly in several courses across the course of my education.

But a path only walked once or twice will quickly disappear. Yes, I studied art history for that one quarter I took the class but I never really revisited that path making it "hard" to recall. I can still get to that information but I might have to rediscover the path.

And, in fact, this happened. When I traveled in Europe in my thirties and found myself in a museum looking at paintings I had studied, all of a sudden little bits and pieces of knowledge popped back in my mind. Seeing the painting reactivated the path just enough for me to get there again.

This is what retrieval is all about.

Focus Facts for Better Retrieval

Typically, we focus on something for one of four reasons:

1. **We are looking for it.** Whether it's hunting for car keys or reading this sentence, you are seeking something and that creates focus and therefore a short-term memory.

2. **It's meaningful to you in some way.** Perhaps it's related to your work and you tune in. Or it involves someone you care about. Or maybe you just bought a new car and now you are noticing the other drivers of that same model. Those are mini-moments of focus too.

3. **You need to take some kind of action.** I can walk into my kitchen and not notice anything, but when I start thinking about what's for dinner, I begin to focus on what's in my pantry and fridge, creating a recording.

4. **Something is surprising, unexpected, or startling.** It can be a mild surprise, like the cold coffee mug. While not a big deal, for a second, it made you think, *Wait. What's up? This shouldn't be cold.* It might be some anomaly, like an advertisement that shows a talking gecko or a friend's completely new hairstyle. The surprise or difference creates focus, which turns on the hippocampus and creates a recording. It can also be much more dramatic, like smelling smoke or hearing a loud noise. Those kinds of events activate the amygdala, which is the brain structure that sets off our fight-flight-freeze response, which floods the body with hormones within 200 milliseconds. When the amygdala is aroused, it instantly turns on the hippocampus to begin recording. This is, of course, a survival response: our species lives longer if we pay attention during life-threatening events because we are more likely to survive them the next time.

10. Retrievals, Not Repetition

One of the biggest insights from brain science has to do with how our memories are made. For conceptual learning, the evidence is clear that it is through the act of retrieval—having to recall something we have learned—that actually makes learning memorable for the long run.

We used to think it was repetition, which many of us experienced during our education. Back then, writing things over and over or doing problems over and over was believed to be the key to learning. But it turns out that it is retrieval, not repetition, that makes the difference. We actually grow memory by strengthening the neural pathway. As that little electrical charge happens, the neural pathway gets measurably thicker. Almost like doing a bicep curl. But it's not processing incoming information that thickens it but rather retrieving the learning back from the brain.

The difference between retrieval and repetition is subtle but powerful. Let's take what you learned about Bloom's Taxonomy of Knowledge as an example. Rereading that section or going over your notes would be repetition, because you are taking the information *in* again. A retrieval would be asking yourself to name the six levels, like a mini-quiz. In other words, you have to look inside your mind and get what you learned *out* of there. If you got them correct, that would be one successful recall. You could ask yourself to define each level, and that would give you another successful recall as part of this retrieval session.

Many studies have proven this, such as one at Kent State University that compared several groups of students that learned the same information and then were tested on that information forty-six days later (Rawson and Dunlosky, 2011). The first group just learned the information once. The second group did one retrieval session with correct recalls and the third group did three retrieval sessions with correct recalls. The groups that did retrieval sessions performed significantly better than the first group, which seems kind of obvious. But note that they were asked to retrieve what they had already learned, not learn it again. Being able to recall the information correctly, and then spacing out those retrievals, had a significant impact on both retention and accuracy.

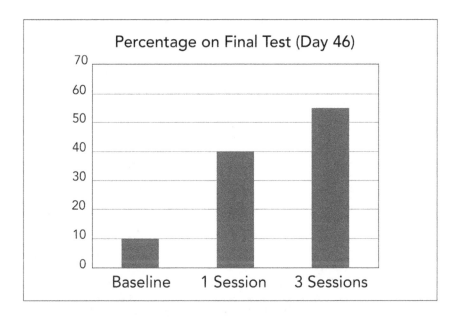

Value of three retrievals

Interestingly, they've also tested whether more retrievals led to even better results but the students only showed minimal improvements after three retrievals. So the researchers' advice to learners is to do three correct recalls per retrieval session and then space out three retrieval sessions over time. The level of specificity depends on the situation and what the learner needs to be successful. For the content in this book, for example, you might want to do a retrieval session on Phase 1 and ask yourself to remember Bloom's Taxonomy, Kolb's

Cycle, and some bits about the hippocampus (that would get you to three recalls). Or you might choose to go deeper and do a retrieval session on only Bloom's model and do recalls of the six levels, higher-ordered thinking, and how it can be applied to something like change management.

You might be wondering if retrievals can only be tests or quizzes. The answer is no. Retrieval can occur through a variety of methods like sharing what you learned with someone else, reflecting on how it relates to a past experience, doing an activity with hands-on application, quizzing yourself on your understanding like recalling answers to flash-card questions, and a host of other typical learning activities. Learning designers can easily build those kinds of retrievals into learning events as well as empower learners to do that for themselves.

Here's another really fascinating study on retrievals: Researchers at South Florida University took college students learning math and they split the students into two groups.

Group A learned math, and that same day, did ten problems using that math. Group B learned the same math but only did five problems. Seven days later Group B did five more problems. In other words, both groups had the same instruction and same total number of problems but they were spaced differently. Then both groups took the same test. Group A, who did the ten problems on Day one got 75 percent right; Group B got 70 percent right.

At this point you might think that doing the ten problems together is the better way to go right? But wait . . . the researchers tested the students again four weeks later, and this time Group A dropped to 32 percent, while Group B held up to 64 percent—twice the performance of Group A.

It's clear that retrievals help with long-term retention. The learning sticks because the path to get to the information is more traveled.

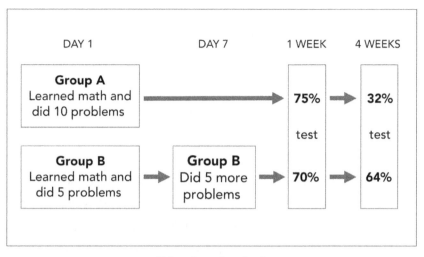

Value of spaced retrievals

Here's another fascinating study that blew my mind. Researchers at Santa Clara and York Universities looked at the timing of the spacing to see if it mattered. They asked a group of students to learn Swahili and English word pairs and then split the students into four groups. All were given the same long-term memory test but the first group didn't do a retrieval session and later they did a long-term memory test. They remembered 50 percent of it. The second group had one retrieval session on the same day they learned the material, but it was twelve hours later, like 8 a.m. to 8 p.m. On the long-term memory test, they retained 55 percent. The third group also had a twelve-hour span of time from learning to retrieval but it was overnight (8 p.m. to 8 a.m.). This group retained 65 percent. And finally, the fourth group had twenty-four hours between their learning and the retrieval session. And they retained 75 percent of the learning.

What's going on here? What's causing this significant difference?

The answer: it's sleep!

Brain scientists have discovered all kinds of fascinating things about the sleeping brain, including the fact that our day's learning moves into long-term memory during sleep.

Vitamin Z

While we sleep, our brain does a little housecleaning, dumping the bits of information and experiences that were not relevant and then moving the most relevant bits into the various regions of our brain, integrating what we already know with what we just learned.

If you have not yet seen Pixar's animated movie *Inside Out*, you should. They actually do a great job depicting this nightly process.

Scientists have also discovered that all of this mainly happens during the stage of sleep called REM for rapid eye movement. In fact, it turns out that last hour of sleep is the most important. The hour right before we wake up is when most of this is happening.

Before I learned about this research, I used to set an alarm and I relied on it to wake up. But using an alarm often cuts off that last hour of sleep, shortchanging this important brain process. So if possible, try to structure your schedule so you wake up naturally, without the aid of a device. I need about eight hours of sleep and I do best if I'm in bed by 10 p.m. and asleep by 10:30. People's sleep requirements vary. Some folks are great with six hours and others really truly need ten. Everyone is different, so you need to learn what is best for you.

When we think about how many people are stressed out, over-caffeinated, and not getting enough sleep, it's no wonder that lots of folks are struggling to remember what they learned. We simply are working against the brain at almost every turn.

Besides helping with learning, sleep provides all kinds of other amazing benefits. Bodies heal themselves during sleep. Cells and tissues repair themselves and the body essentially sweeps out toxins like smoke, pesticides, and other carcinogens that we may have been exposed to. Some medical doctors believe that it is the build-up of those toxins over time that lead to cancer, Alzheimer's disease, and other disorders. A study at Duke University identified that lack of sleep was associated with diabetes, heart disease, and elevated stress levels.

Harvard Medical School has an entire division dedicated to "sleep medicine" and the profound effect sleep has on mood, focus, and mental performance among other things. The Chief Wellness Officer at the famous Cleveland Clinic states that sleep is the most underutilized health habit.

Further, a study published in *Science* magazine estimated that even one extra hour of sleep can boost happiness, especially for people who are not getting enough. Better sleep has been associated with weight loss, enhanced creativity, and better performance at work.

In her latest book *Thrive: The Third Metric to Redefining Success and Creating a Life of Well-Being, Wisdom, and Wonder*, Arianna Huffington details her own journey through exhaustion to a serious medical incident that served as her wake-up call (no pun intended). She now is a major proponent of sleep, offering her employees the opportunity to use nap pods she has on site at the *Huffington Post*. "I am paying people for their judgment, not their stamina," she has stated. She also encourages everyone to turn their bedrooms into sanctuaries that promote good sleep. This includes leaving electronics like smart phones and TVs in the other room as they notoriously stimulate the brain, making sleep difficult.

This is even truer for children who need much more sleep than adults to function well. Their bodies and brains are still forming and sleep is crucial to the natural growing process.

In their book *Nurture Shock: New Thinking about Children*, authors Bronson and Merryman synthesize several important studies about children and they dedicate an entire chapter to sleep studies. Children today actually get one less hour of sleep than children did thirty years ago and researchers believe it correlates with lower IQ, strained emotional well-being, and obesity. If you are a parent or a teacher, consider how you can help children and young adults learn about the importance of sleep, not only for their learning but their overall health and well-being.

Now that you're more explicitly aware of sleep's countless benefits on the brain's functions, think about how you can prioritize good sleep in your own life and help others do the same. More sleep can only improve your ability to learn and retain new things, plus you'll probably be less grumpy.

Take Three with Sleep

Taking the information on retrievals and sleep together, it's clear that for learning it's best to have three retrieval sessions spaced out with at least one overnight of good sleep in between. This is why so many learning designers and teachers are blending online and in-person portions together in different learning experiences. Results are in: having people come together for one long learning event is not effective. If you can break that learning into bite-size, manageable chunks, and space them out, the learning is not only easier to experience, it's more engaging and it will be retained far longer.

Known as blended learning, this process allows me to create a learning journey that unfolds over time and includes three retrievals spaced with sleep. For example, when I design any learning experience, I blend an online component with an interactive experience. Prior to the in-person session (this can be in the same physical room or a virtual meeting), I will have my learners do some preparation, such as watch one of my online training videos on Lynda.com or do some reading. I know that they are likely to sleep prior to the in-person session where we will do a deeper dive with hands-on applied activities. I might build in a light quiz for retrieval or even just discuss it with them. Then I can follow the event with another retrieval, online knowledge check, or an assignment that requires them to use what they learned.

You can use the same principle for your own learning or for learning you create for others.

11. Your Filing Cabinet

Besides retrievals, another powerful tool for moving learning into long-term memory is connecting it to something we already know. Again, research on the brain has illuminated a natural process that already exists: The human brain has a system in place for categorizing what we learn. Much like an elaborate filing system, we have "folders" in our brain where related material gets stored.

Scientists call these folders "schemas" and they essentially are clusters of information. Schemas build up over time through experience as we add to those folders. For example, think of a banana and up will pop its color, shape, taste, smell, whether you like them or not.

Schemas are actually neural networks and they get bigger and stronger as we add to them. Because I traveled in Venezuela, my schema for banana includes the smaller, sweeter *cambur*. And Jack Johnson's song "Banana Pancakes" is part of my schema too, along with fond memories of baking with family. But Jack Johnson doesn't just live in my banana folder—he also attended my college so he's in the UCSB folder, along with the folder of folksy male musicians and people who live in Hawaii.

Venezuela has its own folder too and is filled with lots of memories of my visits there as well as some semi-knowledge about its history and politicians, and the fact that much of its income comes from oil production.

Unlike real file folders, these schemas in our brain can hold an infinite amount of information and make unlimited connections between them. So when I learn something that could be attached to several schemas, it can be added to all of them simultaneously, creating a very rich web of information.

As we live and learn, we continue to grow this neural network. And this process is accelerating with technology. It's estimated that

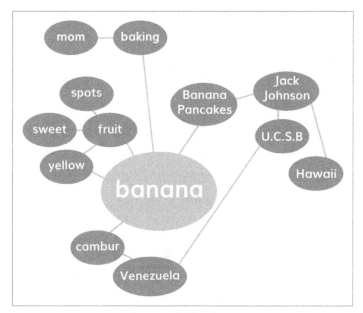

An example of a schema

social media pushes to us 285 pieces of new content per day. Within those tweets and posts are links to articles and videos, which equate to 54,000 words and over 400 minutes of video. And that's just one day! By the end of the week, we can and often do feel overloaded and overwhelmed.

Take comfort in knowing that all of these millions of bits of information have actually added processing time to our brains, which can be misinterpreted as moments of slowness as we get older. Dr. Christiane Northrup, a medical expert on health and aging, rejects the idea that we are having "senior" moments. In fact, she says that we are experiencing the effect of having exponentially more data and memory networks to traverse to find what we are looking for.

As we focus on the learning process, learning professionals can intentionally take advantage of this natural process by attaching new learning to schemas that already exist in the learner's brain. This accomplishes two things. The first is that you can create an insight or an *aha!* moment when people see the connection to something they already know.

The best teachers instinctively do this. Whether they are teaching calculus, software, or leadership, they explain the abstract in concrete ways that connect to learners' existing schemas.

Having been a dean at a major research university, I noticed that this was what distinguished the best math and science instructors from the rest. They were gifted at connecting to schemas that existed in the minds of young adults in a way that made the complex not only accessible, but even easy.

Second, once you hook learning on to an existing schema, it is very difficult for that learning to be forgotten. It becomes part of that stronger neural network instead of being a small, isolated piece of information floating around in the brain.

So how do you activate your learners' schemas? First, you must step into the perspective of your learner. Knowing your audience will help you know what is there to play with. We already have experience with navigating this with audiences of mixed generations. An example that works for Baby Boomers will probably generate blank stares with Millennials.

Any learning design or facilitation should start with you asking yourself, *Who is in the room? How can I make meaningful connections to something they already know?*

Another shift I have made is to share a few different conceptual models or examples instead of just one. This broad approach allows me to activate the schemas of more people in the room since I know that at least one is likely to hit the target. And this approach creates an added benefit of allowing learners to connect the dots between those models.

For example, when I teach change management, I use the Greiner Curve of organizational development, research on the psychological response to change (also known as the change curve), and Dr. Brené

Brown's research on vulnerability. Together, these models give the broader "why and how" change that is both necessary and difficult, and they help leaders understand the intersections at play.

I also ask my audience to remember two times that they experienced change, one that went smoothly and one that was difficult. This exercise then activates those specific memories and their individual schemas of change as well. When I pair this with hands-on activities for leading change effectively, the result is powerful and lasting. This is because I am tapping into the pool of connections that already exists in my (and everyone's) brain.

12. Five Powerful Connections

Research has revealed five types of powerful learning connections that can help move your learning into long-term memory that can be easily retrieved. I like to use a mix of these in my learning events but each may be used individually and tailored to individual needs.

Metacognition

The first connection is metacognition. That's a fancy word for thinking about thinking. Right now you're thinking about learning and how you can enhance your learning process. Another type of metacognition is reflection. This can be reviewing a past experience like a time when learning was easy and fun. Metacognition also occurs when we take an assessment because it helps us see our behavior in a new way.

I love to use a type of metacognition called appreciative inquiry. It's a guided form of reflection where you ask people to focus on their peak performances. You could ask them a time when learning was easy and fun. Or a time when they successfully worked through challenging material. Or even a time they overcame an initial failure.

The goal with appreciative inquiry is to light up the neural pathways of success rather than failure. When we ask people to review times they failed, we light up the failure pathways, which isn't exactly productive and it often activates negative emotions.

So by focusing on peak performances, you can look at what made those times work and build upon those successes. You can ask questions like, *What made that situation different? What worked about it? How can we translate that to a new situation?*

If you want to learn more, I recommend visiting the Center for Appreciative Inquiry's website or reading the book *Appreciative Leadership:*

Focus on What Works to Drive Winning Performance and Build a Thriving Organization by Amanda Trosten-Bloom and others.

Wordplay

Our second most powerful connection is wordplay. Let me demonstrate by asking you to finish these sentences.

I before E, _____.

Thirty days hath September, _____.

Or, for those of you who took music classes: Every good boy _____.

(See answers on page 61.)

These little phrases help us remember things like which months have thirty days or the notes on the musical scale. They are a type of wordplay.

Wordplay moves things into long-term memory because you activate the language center of the brain, essentially connecting learning to the abundant schemas of thousands of words. Acronyms are forms of wordplay where (usually) the first letter of every word combines to make a new word. For example SCUBA (self-contained underwater breathing apparatus), SONAR (sound navigation radar), and SWAT (special weapons and tactics). Mnemonic devices are also connections based on wordplay. They're fantastic because they take a lot of information and package it into something easy to remember.

Here is one of my examples. When I was a senior in high school in the 1980s, I was studying for the AP Bio exam. We had to learn thousands of pieces of information about biology. My friend Ian and I started to create mnemonic devices to give ourselves a fighting chance with all that material.

To this day (thirty years later), I still remember that the names of fungi can be unlocked with this device: Orange Zebras Always Bite Dried Fruit. It stands for "oomycetes, zygomycetes, ascmycetes, basidiomycete, deuteromycetes = fungi." And to this day I remember how much we laughed as we came up with it. That thing is still in my brain all these years later, even though I don't need that information. But my mnemonic device unlocks it every time because it's tapping into the rich language center that happens in our brains.

As a learning designer, use wordplay to create fun ways for your learners to remember information. Or, more importantly, teach them the value of this type of connection so that they can create their own, which will be even more powerful in the long run.

Insight

Have you seen this optical illusion before? This version is from a nineteenth-century German postcard. Some people immediately see an old lady and others see a young girl. They are both in this image. Can you see them?

When I do this activity with a live audience, you can actually hear little gasps, oooohs, and comments around the room as people see the missing piece. If you want to experience more of this, search for optical illusions online (I recommend BrainDen/Optical-Illusions.htm).

That thing that happens when you see the image in the new way is called insight. It's the *aha!* moment. The moment when you gasp or say "ooooh!" as the synapses in your brain connect.

Neuroscientist Mark Beeman has done several studies on what happens in the brain during moments of insight. Using MRI technology,

An optical illusion (William Ely Hill, 1915)

Beeman witnessed that the brain showed different activity than when a person is doing regular thinking or problem solving. He found different regions of the brain are involved in insight and saw "a sudden burst of high frequency (gamma band) neural activity 0.3 seconds prior" to the moment of insight (2004).

Insight is powerful because once it happens, it cannot be undone—that moment of learning cannot be lost. You will never be able to look at the image again and not see the hidden picture. Flashes of insight are indestructible. It reminds me of the movie *The Matrix*, and Neo's choice to take the red pill. Once he sees the illusion, he can never go back to seeing the world the old way.

So how can we use insight as a learning tool? Dr. Josh Davis states, "Instructional design should perhaps shift from content delivery to creating the space for insight." This is an important shift in learning. As Alison King encouraged, instructors need to move from being "the sage on the stage to the guide on the side." This means that if we have a choice between taking five minutes to tell someone information or designing a fifteen-minute experience for them to have their own *aha!* moment, we should always choose the latter. The learning will be much longer lasting because the shift of perspective is permanent.

In my own work, I now consider these four ways to create opportunities for insight:

1. **Introduce a range of concepts.** This increases the chance of creating moments where learners can connect the dots.

2. **Create opportunities for people to learn on their own.** When people seek their own answers, it is much more likely to stick. This is where the advent of technology and smart phones can be a great boon because you can give folks a few minutes to seek for themselves.

3. **Build experiential activities that take learners to the *aha!* moment.** Instead of thinking, *What can I say to help them understand this idea?* it becomes, *What can I have them do that will show them this idea in action?*

4. **Give people down time from the learning.** This might be achieved through longer breaks or time between connected learning events. Yes, breaks from learning actually create moments for insight.

I have a question for you: Typically, where are you and what are you doing when you have moments of insight, those *aha!* moments? When I ask this question, people say things like, "In the shower," or "On a walk," or "Cooking." No one ever says, "Sitting at my desk, concentrating." This is because the brain sometimes needs to move attention away from the learning for the connections to happen. Taking a break is critically important for insight so don't ever underestimate the power of a long break or time off between learning events. Some of your best work will happen when you are not working or with your learners.

Social Engagement

We are wired to be social creatures. A big portion of our nervous system is dedicated to reading emotions in others and forming meaningful connections. This skill is part of our survival, so it also has biological components. If we think about the history of our species, our chances of survival were better if we banded together to gather food and fight the saber-toothed tigers.

Even today, people who live in communities live longer than people who are isolated. And studies have shown that having a couple of close friends is an important component of happiness.

We are innately social creatures, and social learning helps us maximize that aspect of our biology. When we learn in a group, a couple of things happen. The social part of our brains turn on simply because we are in the room together. This is the part of the brain that scans facial expressions, tone of voice, body language, and subtle cues. So by learning in community, we naturally activate all those neural pathways. In addition, we know that, emotionally, most people experience positive emotions when they have engaging and interactive learning experiences. This is why we gravitate to and respond well to stories. Even when we hear a story about someone we don't know or may never meet, stories naturally bring together our social wiring with the rich language information our brain holds. Finally, when we learn in community, our brain connects that learning with those people. So when you run into each other later, you are likely to see that schema activated. For example, my friend Ian is forever in my brain's Biology folder and anything biology makes me think of Ian. When schools and workplaces intentionally anchor learning moments to peers, it causes constant reactivation of the material.

When I teach this material in person, I pair up folks to discuss how they can apply the concepts to the thing they want to learn. Those discussions give me and them several neuroscience goodies. First, it helps the hippocampus process that 15 minutes' worth of content they just learned, freeing it up to learn more. Second, the social wiring of the brain lights up as they talk, even if it's via remote technology like video or audio. Side note here: visual is always more stimulating than just audio so I highly recommend things like Skype, Google Hangout, GoToMeeting, etc. Third, when they see their discussion partner later, they will naturally check in about how that learning is going. There will be a built-in reactivation and a retrieval of this material. Finally, if the content of what you are teaching requires people to use the information or skill in concert or collaboration with other people, then they can practice that as well.

Not all learning can be made social but I have yet to find a topic or skill that wouldn't benefit from adding some human interaction to the mix.

Music

The last of the powerful connections is music. Have you ever wondered why you can remember the lyrics to thousands of songs? I know I can sing every Madonna song ever written, verbatim, from beginning to end. Not to mention Sting, Toad the Wet Sprocket, and India Arie.

What music does is actually touch many regions of the brain to the point that musical memory is nearly indestructible. You can even have serious brain damage and you won't lose the musical part because it's connected to so many different lobes and regions.

Do you know or remember *Schoolhouse Rock*? My generation grew up to watching those animated lessons set to a catchy tune. Sing along with me, "Conjunction junction what's your function?" I once gave this presentation to nearly 1,000 people and the whole room burst into the song! *Schoolhouse Rock* was brilliant. To this day, I can tell you how a bill becomes a law, what conjunctions are, and how adverbs work because the songs are still in my brain and easily retrievable. Another brilliant example is the song, "Do-Re-Me" (as in "Doe, a deer, a female deer") from the *Sound of Music*. That catchy little ditty taught many of us about musical notes.

Tying learning to music is so powerful, it has been harnessed as a tool for a variety of therapies, and there are some incredible success stories with military veterans with traumatic brain injury, stroke victims, and people with autism. Here are just a couple of these amazing stories:

One gentleman, Clive Wearing, suffered severe damage to his hippocampus in 1985, making him incapable of moving his new experiences into long-term memory. In fact, his working memory is seven to thirty seconds, so he can meet you and a few seconds later he will ask who you are. It's tragic story because he doesn't know his family or his caregivers. But Clive is a musician, and while he cannot remember his children, he can play every song he has ever learned and can still conduct a choir.

Musical learning can help us with more than just remembering actual songs. It literally can help rewire damaged parts of the brain. Arizona Congresswoman, Gabrielle Giffords, sustained severe brain trauma when she was shot in the head at a public meeting in 2011. The injury caused her to lose her ability to speak. But music therapists starting working with her because they knew that while she couldn't speak, she would still be able to sing. So they used song to help bring her language center back online. As mentioned, musical learning exists in all the regions of the brain so it helped rewire the language part that had been damaged, rebuilding, refiring, and, therefore, regrowing, the neural pathways through uninjured tissue. (If you're interested, there's a link in Resources to a fascinating *ABC News* feature about the music therapists who worked with Congresswoman Giffords.)

Music is even unlocking the memories of people with Alzheimer's disease and dementia. The documentary *Alive Inside: A Story of Music and Memory* shows how Dan Cohen, a social worker, used music to unlock memory in nursing home patients. The film is filled with example after example of people who seem lost in their own minds and within a few minutes of listening to familiar music are animated, talking and sharing the memories affiliated with those songs. In the film, neurologist Dr. Oliver Sacks states, "Music is inseparable from emotion so it's not just a physiological stimulus. It will call the whole person through many different parts of their brain and the memories and emotions that go with it."

Once the music "awakens" them, these people who seemed disconnected to life and themselves stay present and animated for quite a bit of time afterwards. This is because music touches not only parts of the brain responsible for memories and emotions, but also physical coordination or movement. Each song is like a key that opens the door to their whole being again. I was moved to tears while watching this film because my family has been touched by both dementia and Alzheimer's disease and I realized that we all have the ability to use music to help our loved ones stay connected to their real selves.

So music therapy is a very real and useful tool being used to help lots of people with brain injuries, diseases, and processing challenges. But how is this related to learning? Well, we can make learning nearly unforgettable by connecting it to music. One obvious way is to turn the content into a song, much like Schoolhouse Rock did. Once the song is learned, the content is embedded in the tune. Once I learned about this, I immediately taught my six-year-old a song that has our address and phone number. I now know that even under times of intense stress, she will be able to recall that information and get help.

You can also affiliate the learning with a song that already exists. For example, you might find a song in which the lyrics perfectly underscore specific content or the tone of the experience you are creating. You could then make that song an intentional part of the learning experience. Maybe you have people identify how the lyrics are related or how they could tweak the lyrics to be a perfect fit. In this scenario, your learners would know the song's relationship to the content as well as helping them to recall it later.

It's almost like creating a soundtrack for the learning. For example, when I teach change management, I often use the Beatles' song "Yesterday" to illustrate the emotional transition that people go through with change and the resistance that usually arises during the early stages of the change. For this chapter, we could use Barbara Streisand's "The Way We Were" (misty water-colored memories) or Taylor Swift's "Long Live."

You could also be more subtle and simply play the song at breaks, creating an almost subconscious connection between the learning and the song. I think the first choice is more powerful and leaves less room for the connection to be missed. But people who make movies and television use music all the time to alter our emotions without us really being aware of it.

Finally, when teaching, you can empower your learners to use the power of music for themselves. Ask them to create their own personal song or playlist to anchor the learning and make it easier to recall later. When I teach leadership skills, I ask people to create a playlist that is a mix of songs that recall a time when they were their best or inspires them to be their best. This not only connects the concepts to those songs, it also creates an opportunity to retrieve or recall the content later as they put the playlist together.

These five types of learning connections will help you drive learning into long-term memory, both for yourself and those you are supporting on their learning journey. Not every connection works for every kind of learning, so try them out and pick and choose the ones that feel like natural fit for you and the learning you want to do.

Your Learning Journey

Take a few minutes now to consider how you can harness the power of these five types of connections. Look at the thing you want to learn and consider how you might play with each of them and then choose two to try in the upcoming days.

- **Metacognition**: How can you use reflection, assessment, and thinking about your learning?
- **Wordplay**: How can you use word play to make what you want to learn memorable?
- **Insight**: How might you intentionally experience *aha!* moments that will permanently shift your perspective?
- **Social**: How can you make your learning a social experience, such as learning alongside or with other people, or include social elements, such as talking about learning or sharing with others afterward?
- **Music**: How might you use the power of music to make what you want to learn more memorable?

Answers from page 51

I before E, except after C

Thirty days hath September, April, June, and November

Every good boy does fine

13. The Emotional Sweet Spot

The final way to move learning into long-term memory is through emotions. Brain science shows us that our emotions play an important role in most aspects of our lives, and learning is no exception.

Before we dive into emotions, let's first look at the structures of the brain that relate to emotions. The fields of biology, psychology, neurology, and even anthropology have all shed light on our complex emotional system. Let me share with you some important findings: First, the brain has three layers of increasing sophistication. Known as the triune brain, the layers are the reptilian, the limbic and the neocortex.

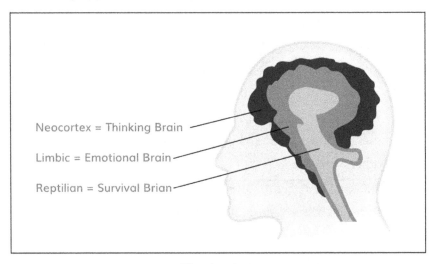

Neocortex = Thinking Brain

Limbic = Emotional Brain

Reptilian = Survival Brian

The triune brain

The most base level is the reptilian brain, which is tied to survival. Through our senses, we are constantly reading our environment for signs of danger. If danger is perceived, the amygdala kicks off the fight, flight, or freeze response and floods our system with adrenalin and cortisol in less than 200 milliseconds. This hormonal flood has a very specific purpose. It quickens the heart to drive blood to the muscles, the lungs expand to take in more oxygen, and fibrinogen and endorphins are released to increase blood clotting and reduce pain, should we be injured. All of these things are designed to help us survive impending danger.

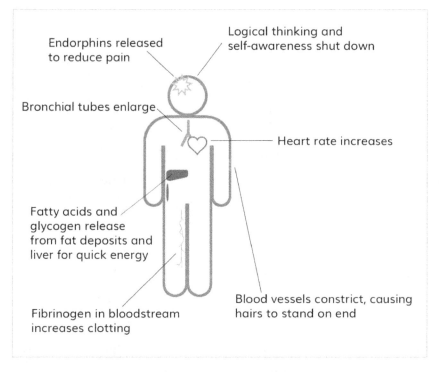

The fight, flight, or freeze response

I'm sure we all can remember a time when we have experienced this. For example, I was driving recently and another car swerved into my lane, setting off my amygdala. It turned out fine but it took several minutes for my heart to slow down and my hands to stop shaking. This hormonal rush is not a pleasant feeling but it does prepare the body to literally escape, hide from, or face the danger.

The middle portion is the limbic brain, also known as our emotional brain. This system allows for more complex emotions than fear or anger. Again, our survival is tied to this portion because we need to be able to connect with others, care for our young, and navigate social groups. This brain sorts for broad emotional categories like happiness, sadness, love, and disgust. This is also where our working memory lives.

The outer portion of the brain is the neocortex, which is our thinking brain, also known as the executive center. It's our highest-functioning state, and where we carry on logical analysis and effective decision-making. Our emotional palette expands to include more nuances and shades of emotions, for example: the difference between calm, pleased, amused, content, and joyous. More importantly, it allows us to have thoughts about emotions and to tune into much subtler indicators than the other brain layers can read.

Both our traditional IQ (intelligence quotient) and EQ (emotional intelligence quotient) live here. Emotional intelligence has four main components: awareness of yourself, awareness of others, self-control, and building relationships. These four areas are further divided by twenty competencies related to personal and professional success. In fact, 80 percent to 90 percent of the professional competencies that differentiate top performance are related to emotional intelligence. If you want to learn more, watch my online training course *Leading with Emotional Intelligence* on Lynda.com.

When our reptilian brain switches on it shuts down other brain functions, including self-awareness and logical analysis. This serves an important purpose: when you are fighting for your life, you probably won't be doing complex calculations, which conserves energy. In addition, if you are injured, your lack of self-awareness will protect you from seeing how injured you really are, reducing your risk of shock.

This would be all fine and good if the amygdala only fired off when we were truly in danger, like during a car accident or a robbery. However, our own personal history shapes our amygdala and what it sees as "danger." For example, I was attacked by a dog in my twenties after being a dog owner my whole life. For several months, my amygdala would kick off every time I saw a dog, even dogs I knew and even photos of dogs.

People can also set off our amygdalas. If your boss reminds you of someone who harmed you, your poor amygdala could be going off in your workplace. And it's generally not good if you lose your self-awareness and logical reasoning at work! This is what is behind good people making bad choices. It's called the "amygdala hijack" and it literally makes us incapable of any kind of intelligent action, emotional or otherwise. Every day, headlines are filled with examples of politicians, athletes, celebrities, and even police officers in the throes of an amygdala hijack.

How does this all relate to learning? Well, if you recall, the amygdala is physically attached to the hippocampus. Data comes in from the sensory nerves and the amygdala takes this information and sorts for safety. If you smelled fire smoke, or if an aggressive stranger burst into the room right now, you would go on alert. And, as we learned earlier, when the amygdala is aroused, it automatically turns on the hippocampus.

When the environment gets stimulating, it says to the hippocampus, "This is important, remember this!" Why? Because it is saying, "Something's going down right now and you need to start recording so I can survive this again the next time it happens." This is why we often remember stressful events with crystal-clear detail. This is true for positive emotions as well. If you found out you just won the lottery, your amygdala would also be aroused and would start the hippocampus recording.

So, we know that emotions matter. The big, powerful emotions like mad and scared and joyful certainly turn on the hippocampus. But other ones do too. Years ago, psychologist Abraham Maslow identified a hierarchy of human needs that are tied to motivation. It essentially comes down to three things we are always trying to do:

1. **Survive**: Our primary motivation is survival. Anything threatening our physical safety is going to arouse the amygdala and turn on the hippocampus. This includes impending physical danger, like a fire, but it also happens if we worry we won't make our house payment or might get fired, because our jobs are how we secure many parts of our physical safety, like food and shelter.

2. **Belong**: When we are safe, we focus on our need to belong. As social beings, we are wired to have meaningful connections with others. This has to do with feeling part of a group and feeling valued in that group. So the amygdala-hippocampus connection turns on when we enter new social settings. Or take a risk in front of our peers. Or perceive that someone might be unhappy with us.

3. **Become**: The highest level of Maslow's hierarchy is about self-actualization or realizing full potential. This is our yearning to grow and become our best self, as well as the urge to contribute to something meaningful. The amygdala and hippocampus will turn on when we feel the joyful and excited emotions affiliated with moments of realized potential and meaningful purpose.

If we think about emotions, experiences can fall on a continuum from threatening and scary to rewarding and positive. We can use the power of emotions to enhance learning experiences. But there is a sweet spot. Anything at the far ends of the spectrum, like the room being on fire or winning the lottery, are going to distract you or your learners from being able to focus on the content you want, or want them, to learn.

And while you can use the power of mild threats (for example, calling on people to speak, criticizing their work) to activate the amygdala and hippocampus, it won't be nearly as effective as using positive measures. To harness the power of emotion to drive learning, slightly positive is what we want to create in our learning environments.

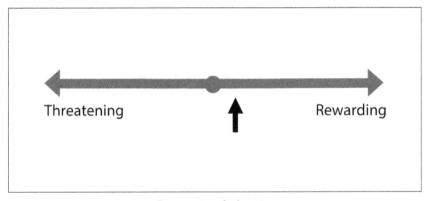

Best emotions for learning

To create slightly positive emotions during a learning event, you have several choices. Consider how you might use the following tools for your own learning or to create learning experiences for others:

- Sharing with others ties into that social connection; try having people pair up for discussions or work in small groups.
- Light competition and quizzes can mildly arouse positive responses as long as they are set up to be safe and not activate fears of failure or ridicule.

- Games and playfulness are great tools. You just have to be sure that they are the right match for your audience and don't come across as childish or cheesy.
- Humor is good too as long as it's appropriate for your audience, and not offensive. This can be tricky because what may seem funny to you might cause an audience member to feel ridiculed or excluded. Be extra careful that your humor creates inclusion and connection for all, and not just some.

Stars of learning design

- Application and reflection allow people to personalize the learning to themselves and their work context, which generally creates positive feelings. In addition, they are forms of metacognition (one of the powerful connections that drives long-term memory) so you get that as an added bonus.
- On-demand learning allows people to find the answers to something they want to know. And learning generated by the learner's curiosity always creates a feeling of success when the answer is found.

- As mentioned, the flash of insight or *aha!* moment also creates positive emotions as the synapses fire and make the connection.
- Finally, we have gratitude and mindfulness, which generate slightly positive emotions in learning, and yield all kinds of other good benefits too, like unlocking emotional intelligence, calming an overactive amygdala, and increasing happiness.

14. Gratitude and Mindfulness

When I present this information in person, people always ask about gratitude and mindfulness. I think most people have experience with the other learning activities on this list, but gratitude and mindfulness are not often seen in learning environments.

Several studies have shown that both gratitude and mindfulness make the brain more receptive to learning. Dr. Alex Korb synthesized some of the key findings on gratitude in his *Psychology Today* article titled "The Grateful Brain: The Neuroscience of Giving Thanks." Studies have shown that intentional gratitude practices boost everything from attention, determination and enthusiasm and reduce things like anxiety, depression, and physical ailments.

Gratitude has an amazing calming effect on the brain and body because it shifts our perspective to what really matters. I weave gratitude into my events by first explaining its power to boost learning. This heads off any confusion about why it is part of reflection and discussion activities. For example, if I am having a leader or manager assess their talent, I might ask them to identify the members of their team for whom they are most grateful. Or, if they are leading a change initiative, I might have them identify the available resources or tools they are grateful for. I often close a session of appreciative inquiry (the metacognition described earlier that is a guided form of reflection on people's peak performances) with gratitude as well.

Mindfulness is a form of focus—becoming completely present to the here and now. And there is strong evidence that mindfulness benefits education. Dr. Patricia Broderick, author of *Learning to Breathe: A Mindfulness Curriculum for Adolescents to Cultivate Emotion Regulation, Attention, and Performance,* details the many positive results for teens and young adults. The Association for Mindfulness in Education uses an evidence-based approach to help teachers and schools implement mindfulness training and they identify at least fourteen key benefits including increased executive function, social skills, and caring for others. In addition, renowned mindfulness researcher Dr. Richard Davidson has been studying the effects of a mindfulness-based kindness curriculum with children. Results showed that the children who participated in the mindfulness program earned higher grades and had greater social competence than the control group (2015).

Anything can be done with mindfulness, from washing the dishes to learning something new. I weave mindfulness into my learning events in two ways. First, I like to begin with sixty seconds of helping people to get present. I welcome them and acknowledge that they probably just came from another meeting or an important task. And I invite them to take a couple of deep breaths so that they can leave all that at the door. I remind them to silence their devices and that by taking a moment to center, they are giving themselves the gift of being here now. I use a calm voice and just encourage them to get present by feeling their feet on the floor and their bodies in the seats. That's it. It can be that simple and not even "woo-woo." Not only can they now focus on what they are learning, they have released or softened feelings of stress or worry, which brings them into the right emotional state for learning. Second, I built some of my activities to be intentionally mindful. I will ask my learners to take five minutes to tune in to what they are thinking and feeling about the content. I may give them a focused activity where they answer prompts or just have a few minutes to free write to gather their thoughts. Whenever we ask people to be in the here and now, versus thinking about the past or predicting into the future, it is mindfulness.

Dr. Richard Davidson's research has really shifted my view of how important mindfulness practices are. His studies use MRIs to explore how the brain changes. He has compared the brains of long-time meditators, like Tibetan monks, to people who have never meditated, and to people who have just done their first-ever meditation. The results are astounding. Even meditating one time permanently changes the brain in a measurable way. And more meditation builds stronger neural pathways, just like any other behavior. People who meditate experience many amazing benefits. They are able to focus longer, they are less likely to ruminate and worry about future events, and when something stressful does happen, they experience less distress in the moment and return quickly to their normal state. All of these benefits aid learning with the "side" benefit of boosting resilience and happiness.

As a result of Davidson's research, I have become a meditator myself. I use the twenty-minute daily meditations from the Chopra Center, which are led by Dr. Deepak Chopra. He has partnered with neuroscientist Dr. Rudolph Tanzi to write the book *Super Brain: Unleashing the Explosive Power of Your Mind to Maximize Health, Happiness, and Spiritual Well-Being*. (See Resources to learn more about this book or Dr. Davidson's articles in *Scientific American* and *Mindful* magazines.)

And I'm not the only one: Jenefer Angell, my editor, wrote a comment in the margin of this page in the manuscript that said, "Amen. I began regular practice after a health scare a couple years ago and I sincerely feel my entire life has transformed as a result." Over the last few years, the power of meditation has come out of the closet with CEOs like Bill Ford (Ford Motor Company), Jeff Weiner (LinkedIn), and Oprah Winfrey revealing their commitment to these practices. Companies like Google, LinkedIn, Apple, and the Huffington Post all offer free classes on meditation and mindfulness to employees because they not only care about their employees' well-being but they know that the company will reap the benefits of a healthier, happier workforce.

Your Learning Journey

Take a few minutes now to consider how you can utilize slightly positive emotions to enhance your learning. Look at the thing you want to learn and consider how you might use each of the following tools.

- Sharing with others
- Light competition and quizzes
- Games and playfulness
- Humor
- Application and reflection
- On-demand learning
- Insight
- Gratitude
- Mindfulness

IV. PHASE 3—DO

Ultimately, the goal of most learning activities is behavior change. Whether it's calculus or leadership or software, and whether the learner is you or someone else, you are trying to elicit new and better behaviors.

While we use the strategies in the first two phases of the model to help the learner take in the information and move it to long-term memory, the third phase is about changing behavior. In other words, changing what we do.

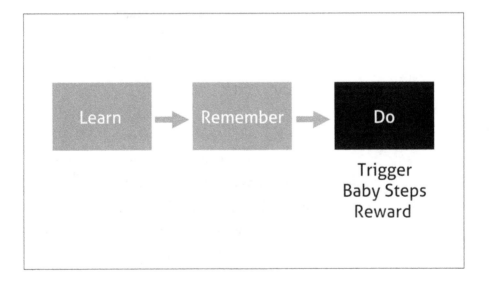

15. The Power of Habit

Charles Duhigg's book *The Power of Habit* changed the way I see my work. He compiled and synthesized the latest studies from places like MIT and Columbia University on habit formation.

We all know habits are formed when we do something so many times that it becomes an automatic reaction, but from a scientific perspective habits are well-grooved neural pathways. Think about how you currently log in to your computer or how you get to work. You probably don't even have to think about it because the brain is running it as a habit loop.

This is actually the function of habits. Learning something new, like how to drive a car or how to use certain software, it takes a lot of cognitive energy. I remember when I was learning to drive: making sure the mirrors were right, remembering the pedals, learning how to shift gears, keeping an eye on the other cars, remembering to signal. It required a lot of attention and focus, which requires the brain to spend a lot of energy. Our bodies have this wonderful biological weapon called the habit, which allows us to take behaviors that we do again and again and move them to a different part of the brain so that they take less energy, freeing up the parts of our brain that do the heavy lifting with new learning.

Naturally, I can drive now without having to spend any energy on mirrors, or clutches, or steering. I can do it without even thinking about it. So how does this happen? It's all the work of the basal ganglia, the structure in the brain that controls movement and reward. Things that we do again and again become condensed into a small little package that move into the basal ganglia, where they can run on autopilot. Researchers at MIT have even been able to see the change in brain activity when this transition happens. Habits are powerful and they are long lasting.

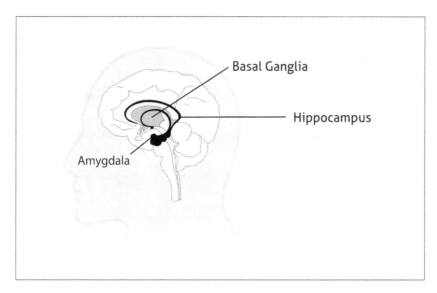

Key brain structures for learning

Scientists have discovered that habits can be broken down into three parts. First, there is the trigger or cue for starting a certain behavior. For example, getting in your car is the trigger or cue to begin the behavior of driving. Or walking into your kitchen in the morning is the cue to begin making coffee. The second part is the behavior routine itself. It's the act of driving—looking in mirrors, turning the steering wheel, stepping on the brake—or of starting the coffee maker and pulling a mug out of the cabinet. The third part, and perhaps most important, is the reward we get for doing a behavior. With driving it's getting to our destination. When I was a teenager the reward included an enormous sense of independence. And for the coffee routine, the rewards might be a delicious Arabica bean plus the caffeine!

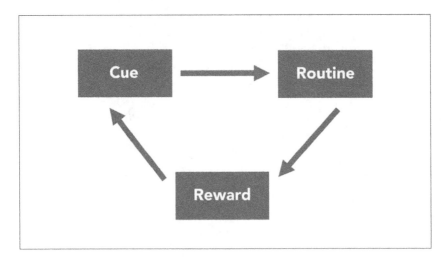

Three elements of a habit loop

Here's the catch: the behavior routine must be compelling in some way to warrant making it a habit. The basal ganglia needs a sense of reward to form a habit loop. Isn't that interesting? And this is where the magic of the research lies. If you want to form a new habit or change an old one, you need to be sure to attach a compelling and immediate reward. When you don't, well, this is why so many of us fail at well-intentioned goals like starting to exercise or changing eating patterns. The reward is too distant for it to compel the basal ganglia to create the habit.

16. The Right Rewards

If you think about it, all kinds of habit loops run in your life every day. And if you break them down you will be able to identify the cue or trigger, the routine, and the reward.

Cue	Routine	Reward
get in car	drive	arrive at destination + sense of freedom
wake up	make coffee	caffeine + taste
order arrives	process the order	make money + please your customer
bedtime	brush your teeth	refreshing taste + avoiding cavities
8 a.m.	start working	be productive + don't get fired
bill arrives	pay it	watch favorite shows + surf the web

Examples of habit loops

You can see that rewards can be positive, like that clean taste in your mouth from brushing your teeth, or avoiding something negative, like growing cavities and going to the dentist. While humans can be motivated toward a positive reward or away from a negative punishment, the research shows that positive is more compelling and therefore better for habit-building.

We have all experienced this. I know in my mind that exercising more will improve my health and help me avoid gaining weight but that doesn't feel very compelling when I am comfy in my warm bed. Duhigg's book helped me make a shift. I realized that in all of the areas where I was stuck, none had compelling rewards. To motivate myself to exercise, I now save the podcasts of my favorite shows and only allow myself to listen to them while working out. Exercising with friends is another good motivator for me.

And it turns out I am not alone. The science of habits can be used to shift all sorts of behaviors. Look at this example from Stockholm, Sweden. Like most cities, they had a problem with people speeding and, like most cities, they were trying to solve the problem through law enforcement and punishments like tickets and fines. Guess how much that strategy changed behavior? Not much. Because driving faster has its own reward of getting the person to their destination quicker and perhaps even a little thrill from not being caught breaking the rules.

Then the authorities in Stockholm decided to use the research on habit design and try something different. They built a new device to sit at intersections. It has a radar gun inside it, and when you come through the intersection, the machine reads your speed and displays it. If you are speeding it gives you a red thumbs down sign, shows you your speed, and takes a picture of license plate, for which you will be fined. Machines displaying speed alone are common in many places, as is the automated ability to catch and punish speeders so that they don't need officers on site and every time. But then they did something revolutionary. The machine also rewards you when you are not speeding. The same machine will give you a green thumbs up signal, post your speed, and though it still takes a picture of your license plate, it also enters you in a lottery to win the speeders' fines!

Brilliant, huh? And it worked. Speeding went down by 22 percent and stayed down. That's a phenomenal, significant result. This shows that the possibility of punishment is only so motivating, but the possibility of reward, even a remote one, like winning that lottery, is enough for us to change our behavior.

As Duhigg shows us, our current habits are not our destiny. We all have the ability to change habits and create the powerful and positive behaviors we want to see in our lives. When you want to change an old habit or create a new one, be sure to build in meaningful rewards.

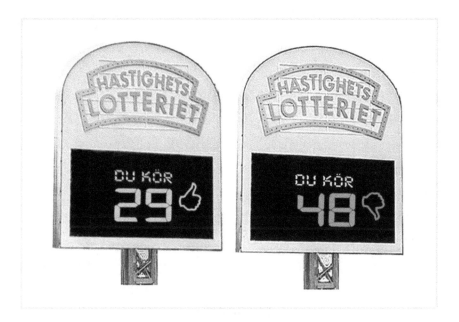

The speed lottery camera (Rolighetsteorin, 2010)

Social connection can be a powerful reward because we respond to acknowledgement and encouragement. Getting that "good job!" makes the basal ganglia very happy. When human skin touches human skin—think high five, pat on the back, or hug—our brain releases oxytocin, a feel-good chemical the basal ganglia loves.

And, of course, prizes, points, and chocolate work too. Duhigg shares one study of a group of people who wanted to exercise more. Split into two groups, both had the same cue (when you wake up) and routine (go for a run). But group A was given a small piece of chocolate when they returned and Group B was not. They didn't do this forever, only until the habit was well formed. But the results were clear. Group A not only formed the habit but participants maintained the habit for far longer than those in Group B. It is also interesting that Group A also maintained the habit long after the chocolate was removed, suggesting that once habits are set, rewards can shift, often becoming built into the activity (once you're fit, running feels good, so the reward now might be just getting out into the fresh air and feeling your body move).

Rewards do not need to be big or showy. They just need to mark that the behavior was done right. And they need to be meaningful to the person in some way. Duhigg's book is filled with stories and examples of people who have made powerful transformations in their lives by working with the habit loops. This can include the obvious choices around health and wellness to how we manage people and how we lead organizations. (Visit Charlesduhigg.com for helpful videos and resources.)

Habits are not just for grownups, either. Dr. Alan Kazdin from Yale University, has applied habit research and design to children and created a powerful parenting method that can shift even the most difficult and defiant child. Many people try to control children's behavior with punishments, not working with the brain's wiring that orients it to habits and rewards. By simply rewarding "good" behaviors, you can create huge shifts in every human, no matter their age.

My husband and I use this method with our daughter. When she was seven, I was near my wit's end because she was talking back, not listening, and generally being difficult. She also was exhibiting some challenges with controlling her anger. We started using the Kazdin Method and saw immediate results. In fact, it was astounding how quickly her behavior turned around. We continue to use this system and I have noticed that all of her teachers in her elementary school use a similar approach. Parents and teachers, I highly recommend that you look at the resources offered by the Yale Parenting Center (see Resources).

17. Creating a Habit

When we are trying to create behavior change, we also need to think about the habits currently in place and how to design new, better habits that will be more compelling than sticking with the comfort of the current ones.

I now think of myself as a habit designer and all of my learning design starts with identifying the habit loop I hope to instill and working backwards from there. To do this, I ask myself questions:

- What words and actions do I want to elicit from people?
- In what context will they need to use them?
- Are any habits currently in place?
- How can I make this new habit easier and more compelling than the old one?

As you recall, habits actually have three parts: a trigger, a behavior, and a reward. When you are building a habit, either for yourself or someone else, there are some important things to know about all three.

To be consistently remembered, the cue or trigger needs to be something obvious, something that people will see or hear. Symbolically, the cue is like a giant "act now" button. A cue should not be an emotion, since those can vary so much in terms of intensity and timing. If you can, it's best to attach the new habit to a habit that already exists. For example, if you wanted to be better about flossing your teeth, you might want the cue to be setting down your toothbrush. It's something that you can see, and brushing your teeth is already a well-grooved habit, so hooking onto it is more likely to be effective.

Cues can be all kinds of things. Here are some common ones to consider:

- Time of day
- Getting to or from work
- Mealtimes or eating
- Turning on your computer
- Getting ready for a meeting

The possibilities are endless and really depend on what you are trying to do. When I help leaders learn new behaviors for managing their people, we tie the cue to the few minutes prior to their one-on-one meeting with their employee. If you are shifting software systems, the cue might be turning on the computer (now launch Google mail instead of Outlook), or processing an order (now go to SalesForce instead of Dynamics).

When shifting behavior the important thing is to break the routine into baby steps. Routines are often long and complex. For example, think about learning to drive. Giving people all the steps at once is a recipe for disaster. The brain gets overwhelmed and they are likely to make mistakes. Each portion of the longer complex routine should be broken down into a small, doable step. In fact, the step should be so simple and so easy that it's impossible to fail. *First, adjust the mirrors so that you can see. Next, position the seat so that you can easily reach the pedals.* And so forth.

Finally, each correct step in the sequence should have a reward, no matter how small. The reward can be praise, a high five, or even a sound, like a "ding" from a game or a click like we often seen used with animals. To see a great example of this in action, watch this three-minute video of a nine-year-old girl learning to high jump. Though this is her first time attempting one, in fifteen minutes of practice she executes a perfect high jump. As you watch the video, notice how the teacher uses cues, baby steps, and reward (in this case a clicking sound) to build a habit from start to finish.

www.tagteach.com/TAGteach_track_and_field

How to build a habit loop

The instructor has built the neural pathway using habit design that clearly illustrates Hebb's Law, which states, "Neurons that fire together, wire together." Donald Hebb, a neuroscientist, noticed that when a behavior or movement is repeated, the neurons along that pathway begin to fire faster and faster. And, of course, that neural pathway will get stronger with further repetition.

18. Repetition, Not Retrievals

As we saw earlier, repetition is not an effective way to move learning into memory. But habits are all about repetition.

There's an old adage that it takes twenty-one days to form a habit. Well, they got the idea right, but the details wrong. Studies are showing that it takes about twenty repetitions of a behavior to start a neural pathway; and by *forty* repetitions it can be considered a habit—provided the right cue and rewards are in place. By sixty-six repetitions, scientists can actually see and measure the neurons getting thicker on that neural pathway.

Remember how sleep helps move what we learned into long-term memory? Well, sleep is also important for habit design, because the sleeping brain does its important work. After sleep, the high jump instructor would want to bring the girl back and run the habit loop again and again. And this is where we can do a better job when designing learning events. If we are building a habit, we shouldn't just talk about it. Learners need to *do* the habit, in the correct sequence to build the right neural pathway.

I can't tell you how many times I have attended a workshop or training or class where the instructor tells us about certain principles, and we might even discuss them, but we never actually DO them. For example, I once attended a mandatory three-day training on becoming a better manager. We were introduced to some models and theories of good management. And we talked about those models in pairs and small groups. But we never actually did an activity that replicated managing people. We didn't role play a one-on-one meeting. We didn't practice delegating a task, nor did we assess the capabilities or confidence of our employees. And since we did not practice a single activity related to managing people, it will not surprise you to learn that, according to answers on the annual employee engagement survey, the program didn't actually shift people's management skills. While the attendees "liked" the program, it didn't deliver real results.

I have gone on to build my own management and leadership programs, and I have people start building the right behaviors and habit loops during the learning event itself. They practice skills at least once or twice while they are with me. And they also get better at tackling real and difficult issues because they work on them in the safety of a learning environment where they can make mistakes.

This idea of building habits can be applied to any professional learning situation. Let's say you're implementing a new software system in your company and you want people to get comfortable quickly. And let's say that they will be using this software twice a week. How many weeks will it take before the habit is built? At least twenty weeks, right? But if you have them use that software five to ten times in the training session, they are well on their way to getting the habit formed. That's a much better use of everyone's time than just hearing about the change and then having to muddle through on their own when they are back at their desks.

This is big part of why 70 percent of all change initiatives fail. Every year, organizations of all types and sizes spend billions of dollars implementing change. But they rarely consider the habit implications for that change, and what it means to someone's currently rewarding, well-grooved routine. There will always be some resistance to change, but a large part of resistance is due to the fact that we are likely asking people to not only start a new habit that is awkward and uncomfortable, but we asking them to give up a habit that is well-grooved and easy.

No wonder people resist, especially because they are usually given little help to make the transition. Leaders can get frustrated with the inevitable grumbling but that grumbling can be reduced quickly if they help people intentionally (and with reward!) build the habit they want.

The length of time people will resist or complain about the change is actually predictable. It's going to be about thirty to forty repetitions. So if it's something that occurs daily, folks will move through it in six to eight weeks. If it's a behavior that they do weekly or monthly, it means a longer, drawn out period of adjustment. Unless you build some of those repetitions into a learning event, or implementation phase, in which case you can shorten the time frame and lessen the frustration.

Duhigg's book also looks at habit change within organizations. The principles apply to work settings and he shares examples of how some organizations shifted the behaviors of their employees through habit design. Think about the importance of the right habits in high-risk work areas like factories and hospitals. Proper habit design has the potential to save, not only billions of dollars in all kinds of industries, but lives as well.

Organizations can also use research on habits to affect the behaviors of their consumers. How people purchase and use products and services are also types of habits and companies are now exploring how they can intentionally shift our habits to their benefit.

Habits are a natural part of our biological functioning and they are at the heart of thousands of daily behaviors around the world. Harness the power of habit for yourself and consider how you might adjust the cue, routine, and reward to build the positive habits that support your success in all areas of your life.

Your Learning Journey

Habit design also applies to the thing you want to learn. Be intentional about building the right habit from the start and giving yourself the rewards that will keep you motivated when it's challenging. Consider these questions:

- **Cue:** What can you use as the cue or trigger to start the routine?
- **Routine:** Identify, specifically, the behaviors you need to do to be successful at that activity. How might you break it into small, infallible baby steps, so that you can build the neural pathway correctly?
- **Reward:** How can you give yourself meaningful rewards?
- **Repetition:** How can you create enough repetitions to quickly get to forty or more?

V. DESIGN

I created this three-phase model because the entire learning journey is important. If we are not diligent through the entire process, we can actually undermine the goal we are trying to achieve, which is changing behavior.

I also believe that each of us is a lifelong learner. I have benefitted greatly from understanding the neuroscience of learning for my own growth and improvement. And I know that in my roles as a parent, mentor, and learning professional, I have used this information to positively impact others.

19. Tying It All Together

Now you have the keys as well. You can harness your own biology—and help others do the same—to maximize learning by focusing, breaking learning events into fifteen-minute chunks, allowing for processing, and being mindful of the learning levels and cycle.

You also know how to move learning into long-term memory so that you can use it in the future. You can design your learning to include retrievals, ideally three, spaced with sleep. You can also utilize slightly positive emotions to work with the amygdala's connection to the hippocampus.

You can intentionally activate the five powerful connections of metacognition, word play, insight, social engagement, and music to make your learning not only memorable, but fun.

Finally, you can take advantage of the brain's natural process for forming habits, by assessing the habit currently in place and intentionally designing a habit that is better and more compelling than sticking with the old way of doing things.

To do this, you can find the right kinds of cues and triggers. You can break the routine into baby steps to correctly build the neural pathway. And you can harness meaningful rewards to shift behavior in lasting ways.

As you made your way through this book and completed the Your Learning Journey sections, I hope you tried applying the concepts to something you want to learn so that now you have a robust learning plan for yourself. It's time to go use it!

Remember, whenever you move from learning to doing, the plan will need a little tweaking but you now know how the brain works and by applying that knowledge you can innovate variations that will work for you.

20. Tips for Teachers, Parents, Managers, and All Learning Designers

For me, understanding the neuroscience of learning has shifted how I approach my own learning and also how I design learning experiences for others. And whether we realize it or not, we all design learning experiences for others. If you are a manager, you probably do some teaching, training, and mentoring with your employees. If you work in health care, much of your work is about educating people on the implications of their choices and how to do more healthful behaviors. Parents certainly design learning experiences. Every day, we teach our children all kinds of information, skills and behaviors. And of course, we teach our romantic partners some stuff too. And then there are the learning professionals, like teachers (from nursery school to graduate programs), sports coaches, music instructors, fitness class leaders, and all those who design training and learning events for a range of employees in working environments.

From a learning design perspective, here are my key take-aways:

1. **Work with the brain to create learning:** Hopefully you now appreciate the brain's remarkable structures and processes, and how they are perfectly designed to help us learn, remember, and do. We just need to work *with* those structures and not against them.

2. **Start with the habit you want to create:** If you start by thinking about the actual behavior you want to elicit, you can intentionally build the habit loop. Once you have that figured out, work backwards to create the learning experience that creates that habit.

3. **Become the guide on the side:** It was an epiphany to realize that I serve my learners best when I step off the stage and support them in their own learning journey. That was a difficult transition at first because it feels good to be the expert and the engaging speaker who makes people laugh and appears to have all the answers. But when I am the "sage on the stage," I actually shortchange their own abilities and processes.

4. **Create opportunities for insight:** Never underestimate the power of that flash of insight or *aha!* moment. When faced with the choice of telling people something in ten minutes or creating a twenty-five-minute experience that leads them to the insight, always choose the *aha!* moment because the learning will be more powerful and longer lasting.

5. **Use the magic of 3:** Now that you've gone through my synthesis of the neuroscience of learning, you might have noticed they fall convenient into three categories of three: Three retrievals of the material, spaced with sleep, designing learning to hit at least three levels of Bloom's Taxonomy of Knowledge (memorization, comprehension, application, analysis, creation, and evaluation), and at least three types of the powerful connections (metacognition, word play, insight, social engagement, and music).

3 levels of learning

3 connections

3 retrievals, spaced with sleep

Blend learning elements
to get there and flip the
classroom

The magic of three

6. **Blend learning elements together:** To maximize the magic of three, blend various learning elements together. We have so many options at our fingertips these days, especially with online and offline opportunities. Explore among the various combinations and choose the ones that best match your content and audience. Just be sure the activities you choose create the slightly positive emotion that arouses the amygdala in a good way.

7. **Flip the classroom:** I have found that the best way to get to three retrievals spaced with sleep is to flip the classroom, which means having people learn some of the basic content on their own through prework. Then you use the instructor-led time to go deeper with that material and give learners the time to experiment and practice. I had the luxury of working at Lynda.com, an online training company, and I was encouraged to drink our own champagne. I built every aspect

of the learning and development offerings to include pre-work that featured one of our thousands of courses. Then I brought people together for an in-person experience, where we utilized some of that prelearning to do a deeper dive, with hands-on application and habit-building specific to our company culture and the learner's context within their function or department. Finally, I gave my learners additional post-work to further develop the habit as well as extend their learning with additional resources.

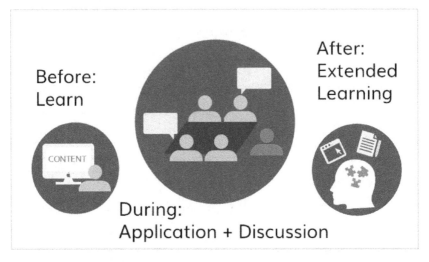

The flipped classroom

8. **Continue to learn about the brain sciences:** We really are on a new frontier of discovery. Every day, scientists from a range of fields are learning new things about the amazing complexity of our bodies and brains, and how each can be used to help the other. We have only begun to scratch the surface of understanding and, with it, the ability to maximize potential. Make a point of staying informed. In Resources, I list some of my favorite sources for keeping on top of the latest findings.

Your Learning Journey

As we conclude, look over your notes from applying the concepts in this book to the thing you want to learn. You should now have a robust learning plan for yourself that will harness brain science to master this skill. It may take a little time, but with retrievals and repetitions, you can learn and improve. Take a moment to finalize your notes and create an action plan that will unfold over the next four to six weeks.

I'll close by saying that we can all benefit from knowing how to harness our biology to maximize our potential. Continue to tend to your own growth and development. You have a lot of unrealized ability within you—we all do. Part of our journey as humans is learning how to step up to that potential and help others do the same.

Thank you for taking this learning journey with me.

Warmly,

RESOURCES & REFERENCES

Brain science is a burgeoning field and within it, you will find a wide range of defined specialties from neurology to psychology to biology. This is a list of some of the scholars, practitioners, and organizations that I follow whose work sheds light on how the brain influences learning and behavior change.

Articles and Studies

"A Learning Secret: Don't Take Notes with a Laptop" by Cindi May, 2014, *Scientific American* (www.scientificamerican.com/article/a-learning-secret-don-t-take-notes-with-a-laptop).

"A Theory of Human Motivation" by Abraham Maslow, *Psychological Review*, 1943, Vol. 50:4, p. 370–96 (psychclassics.yorku.ca/Maslow/motivation.htm).

"Are Mastery and Ability Goals Both Adaptive?" by R. Butler. *British Journal of Educational Psychology*, 2006, Vol. 76:3, p. 595–611.

"Creating a Culture of Learning in Six Steps" by B. Andreatta, *Lynda.com* Enterprise Solutions, Oct 2015 (http://www.slideshare.net/lyndadotcom/creating-a-culture-of-learning-in-6-steps).

"Daily Habit of These Outrageously Successful People," *The Huffington Post*, Sept 27, 2013 (www.huffingtonpost.com/2013/07/05/business-meditation-executives-meditate_n_3528731.html).

"Here's Why, How, and What You Should Doodle to Boost Your Memory and Creativity" by Jennifer Miller, *Fast Company*, 2014 (www.fastcocreate.com/3034356/heres-why-how-and-what-you-should-doodle-to-boost-your-memory-and-creativity).

"How Human Memory Works" by R. Mohs, *HowStuffWorks.com* (science.howstuffworks.com/life/inside-the-mind/human-brain/human-memory.htm).

"How to Train Your Brain by T. Picha." *Mindful*, Aug 2014, p. 51–9 (steamboatbuddhistcenter.org/_/Great_Articles_files/How%20to%20Train%20Your%20Brain.pdf).

"Learning That Lasts through AGES" by L. Davachi, T. Kiefer, D. Rock, and L. Rock. *NeuroLeadership Journal*, 2010, Vol. 3, p. 1–10.

"Long-term Memory, Sleep and the Spacing Effect" by M. Bell, N. Kawadri, P. Simone, and M. Wiseheart. *Memory*, 2013, Vol. 22:3, p. 1–8.

"Neural Activity When People Solve Verbal Problems with Insight" by Jung-Beeman M., Bowden E.M., Haberman J., et al., 2004 (PLoS Biol 2:4: e97. doi:10.1371/journal.pbio.0020097).

"Neuroscience Reveals the Secrets of Meditation's Benefits" by M. Ricard, A. Lutz, and R. Davidson. *Scientific American*, 2014, Vol. 311:5.

"Optimizing Schedules of Retrieval Practice for Durable and Efficient Learning" by K. Rawson and J. Dunlosky. *Journal of Experimental Psychology*, 2011, Vol. 140:3, p. 283–301.

"Music and Memory" by J. Dean. *PsyBlog*, 11 Dec 2013 (www.spring.org.uk/2013/12/music-and-memory-5-awesome-new-psychology-studies.php).

"The Aha! Moment: The Neural Basis of Solving Problems with Insight" by J. Kounios and M. Breeman 11 Nov 2011 (www.creativitypost.com/science/the_aha_moment._the_cognitive_neuroscience_of_insight).

"The Grateful Brain: The Neuroscience of Giving Thanks," by A. Korb, *Psychology Today*, 20 Nov 2012 (www.psychologytoday.com/blog/prefrontal-nudity/201211/the-grateful-brain).

"The Science of Making Learning Stick by J. Davis, M. Balda, D. Rock, P. McGinniss, and L. Davachi. *NeuroLeadership Journal*, 2014, Vol. 5, p. 3–15.

"How to Improve Your Memory" (adapted with permission from Harvard Health Letter) by M. Smith and L. Robinson, 2014 (www.helpguide.org/articles/memory/how-to-improve-your-memory.htm).

"Six Tips for Working with the Brain to Create Real Behavior Change" by B. Andreatta. *Talent Development*, 8 Sept 2015, p. 48–53 (www.td.org/Publications/Magazines/TD/TD-Archive/2015/09/Six-Tips-for-Working-with-the-Brain-to-Create-Real-Behavior-Change).

"The Pen Is Mightier Than the Keyboard: Advantages of Longhand over Laptop Note Taking" by P. Mueller and D. Oppenheimer, *Psychological Science*, 2014 (pss.sagepub.com/content/25/6/1159).

"Using Spacing to Enhance Diverse Forms of Learning" by S. Carpenter, N. Cepeda, D. Rohrer, S. Kang, and H. Pashler, *Educational Psychology Review*, 2012, Vol. 24, p. 369–78.

"Why Teaching Mindfulness Benefits Students' Learning" by Tina Barseghian, KQED News, 12 Sept 2013 (ww2.kqed.org/mindshift/2013/09/12/why-teaching-mindfulness-benefits-students-learning), from *Learning to Breathe: A Mindfulness Curriculum for Adolescents to Cultivate Emotion Regulation, Attention, and Performance* by P. Broderick (New Harbinger Publications, 2013).

Books

Appreciative Leadership: Focus on What Works to Drive Winning Performance and Build a Thriving Organization by Diana Whitney, Amanda Trosten-Bloom and Kae Rader (McGraw-Hill Education, 2010).

Daring Greatly: How the Courage to Be Vulnerable Transforms the Way We Live, Love, Parent and Lead by Brené Brown (Gotham 2012; Avery, 2015).

Drive: The Surprising Truth about What Motivates Us by Daniel Pink (Riverhead Books, 2011).

Experiential Learning: Experience as the Source of Learning and Development by David Kolb (Prentice-Hall, 1983).

Focus: The Hidden Driver of Excellence by Daniel Goleman (Harper, 2013).

Goddesses Never Age: The Secret Prescription for Radiant, Vitality, and Well-Being by Christiane Northrup (Hay House, 2015).

Made to Stick: Why Some Ideas Survive and Others Die by Chip and Dan Heath (Random House, 2007).

Mindset: The New Psychology of Success by Carol Dweck (Random House, 2008).

NutureShock: New Thinking about Children by Po Bronson and Ashley Merryman (Twelve, 2009).

"Promoting Prosocial Behavior and Self-Regulatory Skills in Preschool Children through a Mindfulness-Based Kindness Curriculum" by Flook, L., Goldberg, S.B., Pinger, L.J., Davidson, R.J. (2015). *Developmental Psychology*, 51;1, 44–51. (www.investigatinghealthyminds.org/ScientificPublications/2015/Flook PromotingDevPsych.pdf).

Taxonomy of Educational Objectives: The Classification of Educational Goals (Handbook I) by Benjamin Bloom (1956).

The Doodle Revolution: Unlock the Power to Think Differently by Sunni Brown (Portfolio, 2015).

The Everyday Parenting Toolkit: The Kazdin Method for Easy, Step-by-Step, Lasting Change for You and Your Child by Alan Kazdin (First Mariner Books, 2014).

Flourish: A Visionary New Understanding of Happiness and Well-Being by Martin Seligman (Free Press, 2012).

Shine: Using Brain Science to Get the Best from Your People by Edward Hallowell (Harvard Business Review Press, 2011).

Super Brain: Unleashing the Explosive Power of Your Mind to Maximize Health, Happiness, and Spiritual Well-Being by Deepak Chopra and Rudolph Tanzi (Harmony, 2012).

Switch: How to Change Things when Change Is Hard by Chip and Dan Heath (Crown Business, 2010).

The Gifts of Imperfection: Let Go of Who You Think You're Supposed to Be and Embrace Who You Are by Brené Brown (Hazelden, 2010).

The Happiness Advantage: The Seven Principles of Positive Psychology That Fuel Success and Performance at Work by Shawn Achor (Crown Business, 2010).

The Happiness Hypothesis: Finding Modern Truth in Ancient Wisdom by Jonathan Haidt (Basic Books, 2006).

The One World Schoolhouse: Education Reimagined by Salman Khan (Twelve, 2013).

The Power of Habit: Why We Do What We Do in Life and Business by Charles Duhigg (Random House, 2012).

The Whole-Brain Child: Twelve Revolutionary Strategies to Nurture Your Child's Developing Mind, Survive Everyday Parenting Struggles, and Help Your Family Thrive by Daniel Siegel (Mind Your Brain, Inc., and Bryson Creative Productions, 2011).

Thinking, Fast and Slow by Daniel Kahneman (Farrar, Straus and Giroux, 2013).

Thrive: The Third Metric to Redefining Success and Creating a Life of Well-Being, Wisdom, and Wonder by Arianna Huffington (Harmony, 2014).

Wisdom 2.0: The New Movement toward Purposeful Engagement in Business and Life by Soren Gordhamer (HarperCollins, 2009*).*

Centers

Association for Mindfulness in Education
www.mindfuleducation.org

Center for Appreciative Inquiry
www.centerforappreciativeinquiry.net

Center for Investigating Healthy Minds (University of Wisconsin)
www.investigatinghealthyminds.org/cihmcenter.html

Foundation for a Mindful Society
www.mindful.org/about-mindful

Greater Good: The Science of a Meaningful Life (UC Berkeley)
greatergood.berkeley.edu

NeuroLeadership Institute
www.neuroleadership.com/about

Neuroscience Research Center at the University of Texas
med.uth.edu/nrc

Oxford Mindfulness Centre
www.oxfordmindfulness.org

The Chopra Center "Super Brain" Series
www.chopra.com/super-brain-by-deepak-chopra-rudolph-tanzi

Yale Parenting Center
yaleparentingcenter.yale.edu

Media

"Arianna Huffington Speaks about 'Thrive'" at OC Business Summit
(*Huffington Post*, 2014; www.youtube.com/watch?v=CFd-
JxNcdJX0).

"Drive: The Surprising Truth about What Motivates Us" by Dan
Pink (RSA Animates, 2010; www.thersa.org/discover/videos/rsa-
animate/2010/04/rsa-animate—-drive).

"Empathy" by Brené Brown (RSA Animates, 2013; www.thersa.org/
discover/videos/rsa-shorts/2013/12/Brene-Brown-on-Empathy).

"Gabby Giffords: Finding Words through Song" (*ABC News*, 14 Nov
2011 (abcnews.go.com/Health/w_MindBodyNews/gabby-
giffords-finding-voice-music-therapy/story?id=14903987).

"Having Difficult Conversations" by Britt Andreatta (Lynda.com,
2013; www.lynda.com/Business-Skills-tutorials/Having-Difficult-
Conversations/124085-2.html).

"How Your Past Hijacks Your Future" by Britt Andreatta (TEDx
Talks, 2014; www.youtube.com/watch?v=yXt_70Ak670).

"Leading with Emotional Intelligence" by Britt Andreatta
(Lynda.com, 2013; www.lynda.com/Business-Skills-tutorials/
Leading-Emotional-Intelligence/124087-2.html).

"Memory and the Brain" by Super Brain with Rudy Tanzi and
Deepak Chopra (The Chopra Well, 2012; www.youtube.com/
playlist?list=PLdrUeeBIMbrIIc6FMBKRIJ-zA-KAKxQpB&
feature=plcp).

"Teaching High Jump with TAGteach" (TAGteacher, 2012; www.youtube.com/watch?v=5uPSa--Nlt4).

"The Empathic Civilisation" by Jeremy Rifkin (RSA Animate, 2010; www.thersa.org/discover/videos/rsa-animate/2010/05/rsa-animate---the-empathic-civilisation).

"The Happiness Advantage: Linking Positive Brains to Performance" by Shawn Achor (TEDx Talks, 2011); tedxtalks.ted.com/video/TEDxBloomington-Shawn-Achor-The.

"The Power of Habit: How Target Knows You Better Than You Do" by Charles Duhigg (Columbia Business School, 2013; www.youtube.com/watch?v=0G_beU-SmLw).

"Try Something New for 30 Days" by Matt Cutts (TED.com, 2011; www.ted.com/talks/matt_cutts_try_something_new_for_30_days).

"The Neuroscience of Learning" by Britt Andreatta (Lynda.com course, 2014; www.lynda.com/Education-Higher-Education-tutorials/Neuroscience-Learning/188434-2.html).

"The Speed Camera Lottery" by The Fun Theory (Rolighetsteorin, 2010; www.thefuntheory.com/speed-camera-lottery-0).

Inside Out (Pixar Studios, 2015).

Alive Inside: A Story of Music and Memory (MVD Entertainment, 2014).

Schoolhouse Rock! (Walt Disney Studios, 2002).

Scholars

For further information in neuroscience and related fields, here are some people whose work continues to advance understanding of the brain and how we learn or fulfill our potential:

- Brené Brown, PhD, University of Houston
- Richard Davidson, PhD, University of Wisconsin
- Carol Dweck, PhD, Stanford University
- Paul Ekman, PhD, University of California at San Francisco
- Kurt Fischer, PhD, Harvard University
- Daniel Goleman, PhD, Rutgers University
- Mary Helen Immordino-Yang, PhD, University of Southern California
- Dacher Keltner, PhD, University of California at Berkeley
- Rudolph Tanzi, PhD, Harvard University

Acknowledgements: Practicing Gratitude

I dedicated this book Chris and Kiana and now I get to say why: Chris, you are my soulmate in every way. Your love allowed me to step away from childhood fear into this great big world of abundance and happiness. Kiana, we are so lucky you chose us to be your family. Watching your natural ease and joy with learning made me curious to know more.

This book is the result of the hard work and wonderful guidance of Jenefer Angell (PassionfruitProjects.com), my editor extraordinaire who made this project fun, Pema Rocker (StoryCharmer.com), my longtime friend and soul sister who inspired me to share my thoughts through writing, and Leah Young (lywebdesign.com), my illustrator and website goddess who always makes me look good.

I also am grateful for the exceptional guidance of Jolie Miller and Jeff Layton, who guided all of my Lynda.com courses from concept to release. And of course, they are joined by the amazing content and production team, the incredible marketing and creative teams, and the entire rockin' sales team. We are like family and I appreciate every one of you.

I have been blessed to have several extraordinary mentors in my life. Lynda Weinman, you challenged me to step out of my comfort zone in order to have a greater impact on the world. Dr. Kelly McGill, words cannot convey how much I have learned from you and how grateful I am to be your colleague and soul sister. Dr. Cherie Carter-Scott, you taught me your extraordinary method for coaching and it is the foundation of all my work. Dr. Michael Young, you saw my potential when I was a cheeky, twenty-something grad student and you pushed me to own my brilliance. And Dr. Janice Rudestam, your wisdom and guidance have not only helped me heal and grow, you gave me the tools to help others do the same. My heart is full with the deep appreciation I feel for all of you.

To my tribe of learning and talent development professionals. We are in the business of cultivating the potential of our people and I am honored to share this important work with you. Special warm-hearted thanks to my dear colleagues Lisa Slavid, Michele Mollkoy, Margi Mainquist, Lisa Gates, Dawn Murray, and Melanie Brittle. I have grown so much from our connection.

Finally, to the lifelong learners in us all. Here's to the power of *yet*.

About the Author

Dr. Britt Andreatta knows how to harness human potential. Drawing on her unique background in leadership, psychology, education, and the human sciences, she has a profound understanding of how to unlock the best in people. A seasoned professional with more than twenty-five years of experience working with thousands of people, her research and experience consulting with businesses, government agencies, universities, and nonprofit organizations have allowed her to create powerful solutions to today's workplace challenges. Her published titles on learning and leadership include *Wired to Grow, The Neuroscience of Learning, Leading Change, Having Difficult Conversations*, and *Leading with Emotional Intelligence*. Britt is currently writing several more books. A highly sought-after speaker, Britt speaks frequently at international conferences and delivered a TEDx talk called "How Your Past Hijacks Your Future" to rave reviews.

Dr. Andreatta has served as professor and dean at the University of California, Antioch University, and several graduate schools, where she has won numerous teaching awards including "Professor of the Year." She regularly consults with executives and organizations on how to maximize their full potential, including Fortune 500 and 100 companies.

Britt won the 2014 Gold Medal for *Chief Learning Officer* magazine's prestigious Trailblazer Award for the leadership development program she implemented at Lynda.com. She was also nominated for the 2015 CLO Strategy Award for her work on a groundbreaking performance management program based on the growth mindset.

Britt has been the Director of Learning and Development at Lynda.com, where she designed and implemented professional development programs for all global employees, ranging from individual contributors to executive coaching. Dr. Andreatta now serves as the Senior Learning Consultant for Talent and Leadership Development at LinkedIn while continuing to consult, write, and speak.

To learn more, visit www.BrittAndreatta.com

LinkedIn: www.LinkedIn.com/in/BrittAndreatta

Twitter: Twitter.com/BrittAndreatta